MAXIM GORKY

THE WRITER

AN INTERPRETATION

BY

F. M. BORRAS

OXFORD

AT THE CLARENDON PRESS

1967

PRINTED IN GREAT BRITAIN

TO

PROFESSOR S. A. KONOVALOV

MAXIM GORKY THE WRITER

AN INTERPRETATION

Oxford University Press, Ely House, London W. 1

GLASGOW NEW YORK TORONTO MELBOURNE WELLINGTON
CAPE TOWN SALISBURY IBADAN NAIROBI LUSAKA ADDIS ABABA
BOMBAY CALCUTA MADRAS KARACHI LAHORE DACCA
KUALA LUMPUR HONG KONG TOKYO

PREFACE

WITH the exception of Chekhov, Russian writers of the last twenty years of the nineteenth and the beginning of the twentieth century have been neglected in the West. This is regrettable, because the fifty-six years which elapsed between the Emancipation of the serfs and the October Revolution were a period of immense sociological and political interest and several of the writers who grew up during this time (for example Andreev, Bunin, Gorky, and Kuprin) possessed considerable talent. This book is a critical study of the work of only one of these writers—Maxim Gorky—but I hope that it will arouse the reader's interest in the whole of Russian prose fiction of the last decades of Tsarism. Good English translations of some of the best stories and novels of these years, although less numerous than translations of the works of the earlier writers, are to be found in most large public libraries.

I have chosen to write about Maxim Gorky not only because of the intrinsic interest of his best work but also because, in sharp contrast to his treatment in the West, Soviet critics have proclaimed him at once as a major figure of nineteenth-century critical realism and as the fountain-head of their own socialist realism. The Soviet cult of Gorky, both as man and writer, has had certain beneficial results, most particularly in increasing literacy in the Soviet Union and in establishing a link between Tsarist and Soviet literatures. In this book I have not attempted either to attack or to defend this cult but I have tried to show that there are good reasons why Gorky's work should appeal to a Soviet reader, and good reasons also why a Western reader, from a different standpoint, should find his writings interesting and instructive.

I have not attempted to tell the story of Gorky's life but, where it seemed appropriate, I have tried to relate his experience to his work, The best account of his life in English is to be found in Kaun's *Maxim Gorky and his Russia*. The first volume of Ilya Gruzdev's book in Russian (*Gorky i ego vremya*) is excellent but does not go beyond the year 1892. The second volume began to appear in instalments in the magazine *Znamya* in the early months of 1951 but publication ceased after three issues and the book has not yet appeared in its entirety.

The English translations of Gorky's three autobiographical novels, published by the Foreign Languages Publishing House, Moscow, are excellent and I have on occasion used them in the text of my book.

I am grateful to Professor W. E. Mosse of the University of East Anglia, and to Mr. J. D. Morison, Mr. C. A. Johnson and Mr. M. K. Holman of the University of Leeds who read part of the book in proof and made many valuable comments and suggestions.

F. M. B.

CONTENTS

BIOGRAPHICAL CHRONICLE

(Dates in old style)

1868

16 (28) March — Alexei Maximovich Peshkov born in Nizhny Novgorod (now Gorky). Father Maxim Savvatievich Peshkov, a joiner-upholsterer; mother Varvara Vasilievna, only daughter of Vasili Vasilievich and Akulina Ivanovna Kashirin, owners of a dyeing establishment in Nizhny.

1871

Spring — Peshkov family move to Astrakhan upon Maxim Savvatievich's appointment there as office manager of Kolchin's steam-boat company.

29 July — Death of Maxim Savvatievich, aged thirty-one, from cholera contracted from his son.

September — Alexei and mother return to Kashirin household in Nizhny Novgorod.

1876

January–February — Attends parish school.

April — Varvara Vasilievna remarries: second husband, the student Evgeni Vasilievich Maximov.

1877–8

January (1877)– June (1878) — Attends Kunavino elementary school.

1879

5 August — Varvara Vasilievna dies of consumption. Alexei leaves grandparents' house.

1880–4

September 1880– May 1881
November 1881– June 1882
April 1883– August 1884 — Alexei lives and works in the household of Valentin Sergeev, his grandmother's sister's son, a draughtsman and contractor.

1884–8

August 1884– 7 June 1888 — Lives and works in Kazan.

1887

16 February	Death of grandmother.
1 May	Death of grandfather.
12 December	Attempts to shoot himself.

1888

June–August/September — Lives with the Populist revolutionary Mikhail Antonovich Romas in the village of Krasnovidovo, thirty versts from Kazan.

1889

April — While working as a weigher at the wayside station of Krutaya (now Voroponovo) decides with three friends (the station-master's daughter Natasha Basargina and the telegraphists Yurin and Yaroslavtsev) to establish an agricultural colony and to request land for this purpose from Tolstoy. Goes to Moscow hoping to have a personal talk with Tolstoy, but finds the latter absent on a visit to the Troitse-Sergieva monastery.

13 October — First arrest. Imprisoned in Nizhny Novgorod from 13–16 October on a charge of harbouring the revolutionary Somov. Thereafter never free from police supervision.

December — Makes the acquaintance of Vladimir Korolenko, his first literary mentor.

1890

May–June — Knows the chemistry student N. Z. Vasilev, who introduces him to the writings of Nietzsche, in particular *Thus spake Zarathustra*.

1891–2

April (1891)–October (1892) — Leaves Nizhny Novgorod and makes his first long journey on foot through Russia, traversing the region of the lower Volga, the Don region, the Ukraine, the Crimea, the Caucasus.

1892

12 September — First story 'Makar Chudra' published in the Tiflis newspaper *The Caucasus* (*Kavkaz*). Peshkov assumes the pen-name M. Gorky.

1893

26 October — First critical notice on Gorky appears in the Nizhny Novgorod newspaper *Volgar*.

1896

30 August
Marries in Samara the newspaper proof-reader Ekaterina Pavlovna Volzhina.

September
The Marxist Vladimir Posse writes the first critical notice of Gorky's work to appear in a magazine of national standing—a review of the stories 'Toska' and 'Chelkash' published in the critical section of the magazine *Education* (*Obrazovanie*).

October
First attack of tuberculosis.

1897

27 July
Birth of son Maxim.

December
Two ex-revolutionaries of the eighteen-seventies, S. P. Dorovatovsky and A. P. Charushnikov, decide to enter the publishing industry, and Posse persuades them to make two volumes of Gorky's collected sketches and stories their first venture in this field.

1898

24–31 March
Publication of first volume of *Sketches and Stories* (*Ocherki i rasskazy*) in 3,000 copies. Contents: 'Chelkash', 'The Song of the Falcon' ('Pesnya o sokole'), 'On a Raft' ('Na plotakh'), 'A Fit of Depression' ('Toska'), 'Zazubrina', 'Old Arkhip and Lenka', 'Out of Boredom' ('Skuki radi'), 'A Saucy Fellow' ('Ozornik'), 'Makar Chudra', 'The Orlovs' ('Suprugi Orlovy').

16–23 April
Publication of second volume in 3,500 copies. Contents: 'Konovalov', 'Malva', 'Goltva Fair' ('Yarmarka v Goltve'), 'Of the Siskin who Lied and the Woodpecker who Loved the Truth' ('O chize kotory lgal i o dyatle—lyubitele istiny'), 'The Affair with the Clasps' ('Delo s zastyozhkami'), 'Creatures that Once were Men' ('Byvshie lyudi'), 'Emelyan Pilyai', 'Old Izergil', 'In the Steppe' ('V stepi'), 'The Mistake' ('Oshibka').

7 May
Arrested in Nizhny Novgorod because of his connexions during his residence in Tiflis in 1892 with F. E. Afanasiev and other Social Democrats.

12–28 May
Imprisoned in the Metekh fortress, Tiflis.

1899

29 September–
10 October
First visit to St. Petersburg. Enrols as a shareholder in the publishing co-operative 'Knowledge' (Znanie). Becomes literary editor of the

Marxist magazine *Life* (*Zhizn*). Makes the acquaintance of the publisher Pyatnitsky.

1–8 October   Publication of second edition of the first and second volumes of *Sketches and Stories* and of a third volume. Contents: 'Varenka Olesova', 'Kain i Artyom', 'Chums' ('Druzhki'), 'One Autumn Evening' ('Odnazhdy osenyu'), 'Kirilka', 'About the Devil' ('O chorte'), 'More About the Devil' ('Yeshcho o chorte'), 'My Fellow-Traveller' ('Moi sputnik'), 'A Rolling Stone' ('Prokhodimets'), 'The Reader' ('Chitatel').

1900
January   First meeting with Tolstoy in Moscow.

1901
17 April   Arrested in Nizhny Novgorod in connexion with his part in the student demonstration in front of the Kazan cathedral in St. Petersburg (4 March 1901).

17 April–17 May   Imprisoned in Nizhny Novgorod jail.
26 May   Birth of daughter Ekaterina.
7 November   For health reasons leaves Nizhny Novgorod to live in the Crimea.
19 November–   Lives in Oleiz in the Crimea.
20 April 1902

1902
25 February   Elected Honorary Academician in *belles-lettres*.
10 March   Election cancelled at the instigation of Tsar Nicolas II.
6 April   Korolenko resigns from the Academy in protest (re-elected 27 May 1918).
25 August   Chekhov also resigns.

1903
19 December   Unknown assailant attempts to stab Gorky in Nizhny Novgorod.

1905
9 January   Witnesses peaceful demonstrators fired on by troops in front of Winter Palace, St. Petersburg (Bloody Sunday). Draws up a document of protest.

11 January   Arrested in Riga.

12 January– 14 February	Imprisoned in the Peter and Paul fortress.
27 November	First meeting with Lenin in St. Petersburg.
9–13 December	Organizes help in food and arms for barricade fighters during the Moscow armed rising.

1906

4 January	Leaves Russia.
28 March	Arrives New York, U.S.A., with the dual object of preventing the Tsarist Government from raising a loan and of raising funds for the Bolshevik movement. Accompanied by Mme Maria Fyodorovna Andreeva.
1 April	The Hearst newspaper *The World* attacks the immoral relationship of Gorky and Andreeva and they are evicted from the Hotel Belle Clair.
1–8 April	They find shelter with the Martin family on Staten Island.
June–September	Lives with Martins at their house in the Adirondacks.
16 August	Death of daughter Ekaterina.
30 September	Leaves U.S.A.
20 October	Reaches Capri.

1907

April	After appearance of *Mother* (Mat) and *Enemies* (Vragi) Dmitri Filosofov publishes in magazine *Russian Thought* (*Russkaya Mysl*) article 'The End of Gorky' ('Konets Gorkovo').
1–16 May	Attends Fifth Congress of the Russian Social Democratic Labour Party in London.

1908

January	Lunacharsky arrives on Capri.
March	Bogdanov arrives.
10–16 April	Lenin visits Gorky on Capri.

1909

1 January	N. E. Vilonov ('Misha'), the worker from the Urals, arrives on Capri.
11 July	Fifteen workers arrive on Capri from Russia and the work of Gorky's school for revolutionary propagandists begins.
August	Organizers of school invite Lenin to come to Capri to deliver lectures in the school.

5 August	Lenin refuses and invites workers at the school to come to Paris to hear lectures from Bolsheviks.
17 August	Lenin writes to eight workers at the school from the Moscow district attacking its orientation as 'fractional'.
28 October	Five workers leave Capri for Paris.
31 October	Vilonov leaves for Paris.
7 December	School closes.

1910

| 1–14 July | Lenin visits Gorky on Capri. |

1913

21 February	On the occasion of the three hundredth anniversary of the Romanov dynasty a manifesto is published granting an amnesty to all persons guilty of seditious activity only in print.
27 December	Taking advantage of the amnesty Gorky leaves Capri for Russia.
31 December	Arrives St. Petersburg.

1914

| 7 February | Spectator at the MAT presentation of *Nikolai Stavrogin*, dramatization of Dostoevsky's *The Possessed* (Besy). |

1915

| May–October | Organizes the new magazine *Chronicles* (*Letopis*). |
| 18 December | First issue of *Chronicles*. |

1917

18 April	First issue of Gorky's newspaper *New Life* (*Novaya Zhizn*).
20 April	First article in the newspaper *New Life* (No. 2) in the series 'Thoughts out of season' ('Nesvoevremennye mysli').
December	Last issue of *Chronicles*.

1918

15 June	Last article in 'Thoughts out of season'.
16 July	*New Life* suppressed.
July	Publication of *Almanack of World Literature*, ed. Gorky.

| 4 September | Concludes agreement with Lunacharsky, the People's Commissar for Education, for the formation of a publishing house entitled 'World Literature' attached to the Commissariat. |
| 28 December | Elected to the Executive Committee of the Petrograd Workers' and Soldiers' Soviet, and to the presidium of the committee. |

1920

| 10 January | Convokes in his flat the 'Committee for the improvement of living conditions of scholars'. |
| 15 January | Committee resolves to establish a 'Scholars' House' in the ex-palace of the Grand Duke Vladimir Alexandrovich. |

1921

| January–October | Organizes and heads the 'Committee for the improvement of living conditions of artists'. |
| 16 October | Leaves Russia. |

1923

| May–June | Publication of first issue of the magazine *Dialogue* (*Beseda*) in Berlin. |
| 25 May | Writes to presidium of 'Petrograd Committee for improvement of living conditions of scholars' asking to be relieved of duties of Chairman since he is no longer able to fulfil the duties of the post. |

1924

| 21 January | Death of Lenin. |
| 23 April | Gorky arrives Sorrento. |

1925

| May | Last issue of *Dialogue*. |

1927

| 22 October | Communist Academy declares Gorky to be a proletarian writer. |

1928

20 May	Gorky leaves Sorrento for Russia.
28 May	Arrives Moscow.
15 August	Writes to the magazine *L'Europe* his reply to the article of A. Ya. Levinson accusing him of 'selling himself to the devil'.
12 October	Leaves Russia.
19 October	Arrives Sorrento.

1929

| 31 May | Returns to Moscow. |
| 26 October | Returns to Sorrento. |

1931

| 14 May | Returns to Moscow. |

1932

| 17 September | Fortieth anniversary of his début as a writer. Awarded the Order of Lenin. Occasion marked by foundation of the Gorky Literary Institute in Moscow. |

1933

| July | First issue of his magazine *Literary Apprenticeship* (*Literaturnaya Ucheba*). |

1934

10 May	Membership ticket no. 1 of Union of Soviet Writers (founded by decree of 23 April 1932) issued to Gorky.
11 May	Death of son Maxim.
17 August– 1 September	First All-union Congress of Soviet Writers. Gorky elected chairman. Delivers opening and closing addresses.

1936

| 18 June | Dies. |

PRINCIPAL WORKS

STORIES, SKETCHES, NOVELS, AND PLAYS

1892		
12 September	'Makar Chudra'	*Kavkaz* (a Tiflis news-paper)
1893		
5 August	'Emelyan Pilyai'	*Russkie vedomosti* (Moscow news-paper)
4 September	'Of the Siskin who Lied and the Woodpecker who Loved the Truth'	*Volzhsky vestnik* (Nizhny Novgorod newspaper)
16, 22, 27, 30 October	'Two Hobos' ('Dva bosyaka')	*Samarskaya gazeta* (a Samara news-paper)
23, 29, 31 December	'He Ran Off' ('Ubezhal')	*Volgar* (a Nizhny Nov-gorod newspaper)
1894		
13, 16, 18, 20, 23 February (written 1893)	'Old Arkhip and Lenka' ('Ded Ark-hip i Lenka')	*Volgar*
8 April–6 July	*Paul the Wretched* (*Pavel Goryomyka*)	*Volgar*
11, 15, 16, 25, 29, 31 December	'My Fellow-Traveller' ('Moi sputnik')	*Samarskaya gazeta*
1895		
22, 26 January	'At the Salt Marsh' ('Na soli')	*Samarskaya gazeta*
26 February	'The Trotting Ordeal' ('Vyvod')	*Samarskaya gazeta*
16, 23, 27 April (writ-ten autumn 1894)	'Old Izergil' ('Starukha Izergil')	*Samarskaya gazeta*
2 April	'On a Raft' ('Na plo-takh')	*Samarskaya gazeta*
June (written summer 1894)	'Chelkash'	*Russkoe bogatstvo* (magazine)
2, 7 July	'The Affair with the Clasps' ('Delo s zas-yozhkami')	*Samarskaya gazeta*

20, 22 July	'One Autumn Evening' ('Odnazhdy osenyu')	*Samarskaya gazeta*
September	'The Mistake' ('Oshibka')	*Russkaya mysl* (magazine)
1896		
June	'An Attack of Depression' ('Toska')	*Novoe slovo* (magazine)
1897		
March (written second half 1896)	'Konovalov'	*Novoe slovo*
,,	'In the Steppe' ('V stepi')	*Zhizn yuga* (magazine) (supplement no. 1)
11 May	'Zazubrina'	,,
14 May (written 1896)	'Boles'	*Nizhegorodsky listok* (a Nizhni newspaper)
13, 20, 27 April	'Vanka Mazin'	*Zhizn yuga*
20 July	'Goltva Fair' ('Yarmarka v Goltve')	*Nizhegorodsky listok*
August	'A Saucy Fellow' ('Ozornik')	*Severny vestnik* (magazine)
October	'The Orlovs' ('Suprugi Orlovy')	*Russkaya mysl*
October, November	'Creatures that Once were Men' ('Byvshie lyudi')	*Novoe slovo*
November, December	'Malva'	*Severny vestnik*
25 December	'Out of Boredom' ('Skuki radi')	*Samarskaya gazeta*
1898		
March–May	'Varenka Olesova'	*Severny vestnik*
24–31 March	First volume of collected *Sketches and Stories* (*Ocherki i rasskazy*)	
16–23 April	The same. Second vol.	
May–June	'A Rolling Stone' ('Prokhodimets')	*Zhizn* (magazine)
November (written 1895)	'The Reader' ('Chitatel')	*Cosmopolis* (magazine)

1899		
January	'Kain i Artyom'	*Mir bozhi* (magazine)
"	'Kirilka'	*Zhizn*
February	'More About the Devil' ('Yeshcho o chorte')	"
February, March, April, June, July, August, September	*Foma Gordeev*	"
December	'Twenty-six Men and a Girl' ('Dvadtsat shest i odna')	"
1901		
April	'Song of the Stormy Petrel' ('Pesyna o burevestnike')	*Zhizn*
December (written second half of 1900–January 1901)	*The Three of Them* (*Troe*)	Vol. 5 of Gorky's *Tales* published by 'Knowledge'
1902		
18 December (written January —April)	*The Lower Depths* (*Na dne*)	*Première* given by Moscow Arts Theatre
1903		
1 March	'Man' ('Chelovek')	First 'Knowledge' *Miscellany* for 1903
1905		
27 November	'Still More About the Devil' ('I yeshcho o chorte')	*Borba* No. 1 (Marxist newspaper)
1906		
December (first part finished September, second December)	*Mother* (*Mat*) (beginning of Part 1) (in English)	*Appleton's Magazine*, New York
1907		
January/February	*Mother* (remainder of Part 1)	*Appleton's Magazine*
March–July	*Mother* (Part 1)	16th, 17th, and 18th 'Knowledge' *Miscellanies*

April	*Mother*	American edition published by D. Appleton and Co., New York
June	*Mother* (in Russian and German)	Published by I. Ladyzhnikov, Berlin
19 October	*Mother* (beginning of Part 2)	19th 'Knowledge' *Miscellany*
1908		
20 February	*Mother* (Part 2 continued)	20th 'Knowledge' *Miscellany*
9 April	*Mother* (concluded)	21st 'Knowledge' *Miscellany*
27 June	*Confession* (*Ispoved*)	23rd 'Knowledge' *Miscellany*
1909		
December	'Okurov Town' ('Gorodok Okurov')	Published by I. Ladyzhnikov (Berlin)
1910		
May	*The Life of Matvei Kozhemyakin* (Part 1) (*Zhizn Matveya Kozhemyakina*)	30th and 31st 'Knowledge' *Miscellanies*
1911		
8 February (finished September 1910)	*Vassa Zheleznova*	Première given by Nezlobin's theatre, Moscow
March	*The Life of Matvei Kozhemyakin* (Part 2)	35th 'Knowledge' *Miscellany*
16 September	The same (Part 3)	36th 'Knowledge' *Miscellany*
12 November	The same (Part 4)	37th 'Knowledge' *Miscellany*
1912		
17 May	'The Birth of a Man' ('Rozhdenie cheloveka') 'An Incident in the Life of Makar' ('Sluchai iz zhizni Makara')	Published together in one volume by Ladyzhnikov (Berlin) ('Rozhdenie cheloveka' had appeared in Russian in April issue (no. 1) of magazine 'Legacy' (*Zavety*)

1913		
April (1912)– July 1913	*Through Russia (Po Rusi)*	Eleven first sketches of this cycle in various magazines
May	'The Boss' ('Khozyain')	*The Contemporary (Sovremmenik)* magazine
25 August– 30 January 1914	*Childhood (Detstvo)*	*The Russian Word (Russkoe slovo)* a newspaper
1916		
January–December	*My Apprenticeship (V lyudakh)*	Chronicles (*Letopis*)
1917		
November (1915)– June 1917	*Through Russia*	Remaining eighteen sketches published in various magazines
1919		
November (worked on 1918–19)	'Memories of Lev Tolstoy' ('Vospominaniya o Lve Nikolaieviche Tolstom')	Published by Z. I. Grzhebin, St. Petersburg
1923		
January–December	Autobiographical tales ('The Days of Korolenko', 'V. G. Korolenko', 'On the Harm of Philosophy', *My Universities*, 'The Watchman', 'First Love'—'Vremya Korolenko', 'V. G. Korolenko', 'O vrede filosofii', *Moi universitety*, 'Storozh', 'O pervoi lyubvi')	In the magazine *Red Virgin Soil (Krasnaya Nov)*, Nos. 1–6, 1923
1924		
February (written end of 1922–August 1923)	*Notes from My Diary. Recollections (Zametki iz dnevnika. Vospominaniya)*	Published in Berlin by the 'Book' (Kniga) publishing house

1925

| April | Stories 1922–4 (include 'The Story of a Hero' and 'Kara-mora') | 'Book' (Berlin) |
| December–January (1926) | *The Artomonov Business* (*Delo Artomo-novykh*) | 'Book' (Berlin) |

1927

| | *The life of Klim Sam-gin* (*Zhizn Klima Samgina*), Part 1 | 'Book' (Berlin) |

1928

| April | Ibid. (Part 2) | Ibid. |

1931

| February | Ibid. (Part 3) | Ibid. |

1933

| 6 November (written 1932) | *Yegor Bulychov and the Others* (*Yegor Bulychov i drugie*) | Première by Leningrad State theatre |

1936

| April (written 1935) | *Vassa Zheleznova* (second version) *The life of Klim Sam-gin*, Part 4 (unfinished) | Year XIX (*Almanack*, No. 9) |

ARTICLES AND ESSAYS

1896

| 28 February | 'One More Poet' ('Yeshcho poet') | *Samarskaya gazeta* |
| 13, 18 April | 'Paul Verlaine and the Decadents' ('Pol Verlen i dekadenty') | Ibid. |

1900

| 5 January | 'Cyrano de Bergerac' (heroic comedy by Edmond Rostand) | *Nizhegorodsky listok* |

1901		
9 November	'Before Sunrise' (a drama by G. Hauptmann)	Ibid.
1905		
27, 30 October, 13, 20 November	'Notes on the Petty Bourgeois Mentality' ('Zametki o meshchantsve')	*Novaya zhizn* (first legal Bolshevik newspaper)
1908		
27 March	'On Cynicism' ('O tsinisme')	*Literary Decadence.* (*Literaturnoe dekadentsvo*) a critical miscellany
1909		
April	'The Destruction of Personality'	*Essays on the philosophy of collectivism*
	('Razrushenie lichnosti')	(*Miscellany*)
1911		
2 July	'On Balzac'	*La Revue*, No. 14
December–November (1912)	'From Afar' ('Izdaleka'), a series of articles	*The demands of life* (*Zaprosy zhizni*) a weekly
1913		
22 September	'On Karamazovism' ('O Karamazovshchine')	*Russkoye slovo* a newspaper
27 October	'More about Karamazovism' ('Yeshcho o Karamazovshchine') —an open letter	Ibid.
1914		
17 July (written 1897)	'Aleksei Maximovich Peshkov, pen-name Maxim Gorky' (autobiographical sketch)	*Twentieth-century Russian literature,* Vol. 1 (*Russkaya literatura XX veka*), ed. S. A. Vengerov
1915		
18 December	'Two Souls' ('Dve dushi')	*Chronicles (Letopis)*

1917

18 April	'Revolution and Culture' ('Revolyutsia i kultura')	*New Life* (*Novaya Zhizn*), No. 1 newspaper
20 April–15 June (1918)	'Thoughts Out of Season' ('Nesvoevremennye mysli')	*New Life*

1920

20 July	'Vladimir Ilich Lenin'	*The Communist International* (*Kommunistichesky Internatsional*) magazine

1922

6 July	'The Intelligentsia and the Revolution' ('Intelligentsia i revolyutsia')	*Manchester Guardian Commercial*
August	'On the Russian Peasantry' ('O Russkom krestyanstve')	Ladyzhnikov (Berlin)

1923

April	'Le groupe des Freres Serapion'	*Le disque vert* (Paris–Brussels)

1928

7 October	'To the "Mechanical Citizens" of the USSR' ('Mekhanicheskim grazhdanam SSSR')	*Pravda* and *Izvestiya*
27 October	'More about the "Mechanical Citizens"'	*Pravda* and *Izvestiya*

1929

March	'On the Petty Bourgeois Mentality' ('O meshchanstve')	*Na literaturnom postu* magazine

1930

November/December	'Chats about my Craft' ('Besedy o remesle'), No. 1	*Literary Apprenticeship*, No. 6 (*Literaturnaya ucheba*) magazine

December	'How I Write' ('Kak ya pishu')	*How we write* (a miscellany)

1931

January/February	'Chats about my Craft', No. 2	*Literary Apprenticeship*, No. 7
May/June	'Chats about my Craft', No. 3	Ibid. (No. 9)

1933

May	'On Plays' ('O pesakh')	Year XVI (God XVI) *Almanack*, No. 1

1934

18 August	Opening address at the First All-union Congress of Soviet Writers	*Pravda*
19 August	'Soviet Literature' (paper given at the Congress)	*Pravda*

1935

30 January	'On Fairy-tales' ('O skazkakh')	*Pravda*

INTRODUCTORY

I

By the end of the eighteen-sixties in Russia the new forms of social life created by the Emancipation of the serfs and the Great Reforms enacted in the first half of the decade were beginning to take shape. The radical intelligentsia had demanded these reforms in the name of the liberation of the Russian people from the fetters of the past; but the measures enacted were less calculated to satisfy such idealism than to strengthen Tsarism by setting Russia firmly on the road to transformation from the backward, patriarchal state which the disasters of the Crimean War had revealed her to be, into an efficient national economic unit, based upon a flourishing nineteenth-century, capitalistic industrial system. Throughout Russian life, after the enactment of the reforms, the progressive section of the bureaucracy sought to destroy, as rapidly as possible, those survivals of the old way of life which hindered the development of the new; Russian social life, in consequence, in the second half of the nineteenth century, presents a picture of two simultaneous processes of growth and decay, each progressing at a great pace but with the vitality of the new matched in many spheres by the tenacity of the old, so that, even as late as 1917, both in the forms of life and in the mentality of the population, in Sumner's words, 'old features of the serf regime lived on, even if decaying, side by side with the new capitalistic development'.

Since the old patriarchal way of life had been centred on the countryside, it was naturally there that the results of the dual process of growth and decay were the most far-reaching. The new economic system, based on a money economy and mobile, hired labour, revealed to many landowners the naked fact of their bankruptcy, caused by generations of indolence and mismanagement, which under the old system of labour services they had been able to conceal, even from themselves. In the initial period of crisis which followed the Emancipation (1861) such landowners were often obliged to use the land redemption payments, which they received under its terms, to pay off old debts instead of to reorganize their estates in accordance with the new conditions of social and economic life. They would then sell their land to urban merchants or *entrepreneurs* and look for employment in the new institutions of rural management created by the reforms; or leave the countryside altogether to become civil servants or occupy administrative posts in the new industries situated in the towns. Some of them left the countryside without selling their estates and would at most return to inhabit their old houses for a few months in the summer—such estates came to present a melancholy spectacle of neglect and dilapidation.

A small minority of the old landowners, with their estates mostly in the southern Black Earth zone, where the land was fertile enough to make large-scale farming with free hired labour profitable, successfully reorganized their affairs and made a comfortable living from cultivating part of their land and letting off the rest to the peasants, often at exorbitant rents. Even these, however, found that they were no longer, as in the past, the undisputed masters of rural life, but had to share their power and influence with officials of peasant 'self-government' or with representatives of the rising commercial classes who had acquired many of the old estates; the power of the latter was often supported by energetic ex-serfs, who, as small businessmen in the new economic conditions, found many ways of enriching themselves at the expense of their old comrades.

The emancipated peasantry, as a class, underwent an even more radical process of disintegration and differentiation than their old masters. The conditions of the Emancipation provided that the peasants might, if they chose, accept only one quarter of the land due to them and obtain therewith immediate complete freedom; if, on the other hand, they wished to claim their full share of land, they were obliged to pay the Government for it in the form of redemption dues which went to the Exchequer which had already indemnified the landowners with a once-for-all bond issue. The result of this condition was that in the Black Earth zone the peasants often received much less land than was necessary to maintain their large families; and in the Northern Zone they were obliged to pay what amounted to a personal ransom which strained the meagre income they made from agricultural and non-agricultural sources. Liberty, therefore, for thousands of peasants meant poverty: and other conditions of the Emancipation conspired to make even this imperfect liberty no more than a synonym for a change of masters.

The emancipated peasant, if he took his full share of land, did not obtain full private ownership of it, but held it through the village commune—the *mir*—which, if it so desired, could redistribute peasant land from one individual family to another. In addition to this administration of land the *mir* also bore the responsibility for the collection of redemption dues from the peasants, and in consequence, since redemption was a collective responsibility, exercised considerable influence upon the freedom of action of its members. The *mir* in fact occupied a very special position in post-Emancipation rural life. Its power before 1861 had been considerable (it was responsible, for example, for the collection of taxes and the provision of military recruits), but the conditions of the Emancipation greatly increased this power. It was the intention of the authorities that the *mir* should tie the peasants to their holdings until all redemption dues had been met; by this means also they were kept at the disposal of the landlords as agricultural labourers.

Many peasants, in order to meet the taxes, *zemstva* rates, and redemption dues levied on their land, attempted to flee to the towns in search of work in industry, and in certain districts the *mir*, assisted by the local authorities, tried to prevent this migratory movement by force. In Chernigov province, for example, the peasants were tied to their ploughs to oblige them to work and to stop them from running away and forming a wandering proletariat.

In addition to administering the land and collecting redemption dues, it was also the theoretical responsibility of the *mir* to maintain a certain equality among the emancipated peasants. Before 1861 this equality had been maintained almost as part of the natural course of events, firstly by the general economic stagnation and secondly by the omnipotent intervention of the landowners themselves who, in general, did not approve of some of their serfs becoming rich at the expense of others and not only prevented the more energetic of them from acquiring excessive wealth but preserved others from bankruptcy. (A few landowners, among them the mighty Count Sheremetev who just before the Emancipation owned more than 300,000 serfs and upon whose estates later grew up the industrial town of Ivanovo, took the opposite view and prided themselves upon owning serfs who like the Morozov family (once serfs of a landowner named Ryumin) became wealthy merchants.) After 1861 the egalitarian responsibilities of the landowners should have been borne by the *mir*, but the latter, with the introduction of the money factor into village affairs, could not frustrate the abilities of the more astute peasants for self-enrichment; often, indeed, wealthy peasants seized controlling influence in the *mir* and made it their tool. Such men had usually acquired through petty trade enough money with which to buy land from the landowners outside the *mir* or to embark upon more ambitious and more lucrative forms of commercial activity such as money-lending and horse-hiring: as a reference to the amount of money they grabbed from the village population, they came to be known as *kulaki* (fists), and their wealth and power offered a sharp contrast to the wretched condition of the majority of their ex-comrades—starved of land, burdened with dues and taxes, and a prey to the whims of police and bureaucrats. In conditions of extreme poverty some unfortunates would be obliged to sell even their livestock to more prosperous neighbours, thus accelerating the process of economic differentiation in the countryside.

A further feature of post-Emancipation rural Russian life added to the difficulties of the peasantry—the break-up of the old unit of work and ownership, the joint family. After 1861 both moral and economic factors contributed to the rapid disintegration of these units in which three generations had lived and worked together, sometimes attaining a considerable degree of prosperity. Before the Emancipation these families remained largely undivided, because the patriarchal authority of their heads reflected that of the squire himself, and also because the squires appreciated the value of large units of labour and where necessary used their influence to prevent their disintegration. The economic security of these families was often based upon the cottage industries (such as weaving, bootmaking, and pottery) which they had practised from time immemorial. Since the eighteenth century, middlemen had begun to operate these crafts, but after 1861 urban *entrepreneurs* saw in their capitalization an opportunity to make very large profits at little risk and used the defenceless peasants as ill-paid employees. In addition to this, with the removal of the moral authority of the landowner, that of the head of the joint family was gravely weakened, and in a very short time the younger male members of the household conceived the ambition of extending the principle of emancipation to their own lives, and set up in houses and business of their own. The consequent disintegration of the family intensified the poverty of all its members. To quote MacKenzie Wallace: 'Much money had to be expended on constructing new houses and farmsteads: the old habit of one male member remaining at home to cultivate the land allotment with the female members, while the others earned wages elsewhere, had to be abandoned. Many large families, rich by peasant standards, dissolved into three or four small ones on the brink of pauperism.'

In the second half of the nineteenth century there was a sharp increase in the birth-rate among the Russian peasantry and rural population multiplied beyond any possible corresponding addition to land under cultivation. This caused greater suffering than any of the conditions of the Emancipation, and peasants left their homes in thousands in search of food and work in the towns.

It is not surprising that in the conditions of post-Emancipation Russian rural life the peasantry should have become a focal point of unrest and discontent. At first they refused to believe that the terms of the Emancipation, as published, were the real ones, and lived in a constant state of expectancy of the revelation of the true edict. Risings and disturbances during the first half of the sixties were widespread, only to subside for twenty years until the eighties, when indiscipline and drunkenness became so common that, on the demand of the other sections of the rural population, the Government in 1889 created the Land Captains, high-ranking rural officials with both administrative and judicial powers over the peasantry, to keep order. The peasant, indeed, in post-emancipation Russia remained a social and political half-caste, a 'semi-personality' in the words of the Procurator of the Holy Synod, Pobedonostsev. There was no legal demarcation of his rights and duties and he was therefore at the mercy of every representative of the executive power. In judicial matters he was treated differently from the rest of the population, for the rural canton courts were empowered to judge minor civil disputes, involving only peasants, on principles different from those applied to the rest of the nation. Until 1904 these courts could order a peasant to be flogged.

Peasant protest against their hardships, as we have said, found expression in hooliganism and drunkenness: among the better elements of the peasantry, however, discontent motivated adherence to the religious sects which gained in influence during the seventies and eighties. The spiritual power of these sects represented in some degree a moral protest which harmonized with the protests of the patriarchal Tolstoy against the iniquities of the new Russian society which grew up in the second half of the nineteenth century.

The impoverishment of the countryside and the rapid disintegration of the old patriarchal way of rural life is paralleled in late nineteenth-century Russia by the expansion of the towns and the development of urban industry, managed by a new industrial middle class and staffed by a rapidly growing proletariat. Many landowners, as we have seen, joined the management of the new enterprises, and their former serfs who also left their rural homes joined the already existing army of town-bred workmen to form the new proletariat. Naturally, the radical wholesale transformation of Russian social life, of which the decline of the countryside and the growth of the towns were opposite faces, did not take place without much human suffering. Thousands of simple people were uprooted from ways of life which their ancestors had followed for centuries and hurled into the maelstrom of a new, half-formed existence in which many could find no secure place, or, if they did find a corner, found that the process of settling down in it meant the abandonment of values formed by the experience of many generations and the destruction of a personality which was rooted in a way of life rapidly disintegrating. Those peasants who became urban workers were at first despised by the hereditary townsmen whom they joined, who referred to them contemptuously as 'grey'. The employers, intent on making huge profits, exploited mercilessly both the urban workmen and the new arrivals from the countryside; for the first twenty years after the Emancipation the former remained the drunken boors that old Russian life had made them and the latter, retaining patriarchal habits of thought, referred to their employers as 'barin' (squire) and brought to the hardships of industrial life the same spirit of passive resistance with which they had endured rural deprivation and the natural calamities which destroyed their crops. Employers often opposed Governmental interference in their relations with their workers by invoking the principle of patriarchal infallibility. As time passed, the excesses of the employers led to the emergence of a class-consciousness among their workers, based on common interests, and the first Russian Trade Union, the Moscow Workers' Union, was founded by the carpenter Stepan Khalturin in 1879; the type of the working man began slowly to improve, the hereditary townsman taking thought how to better his lot instead of merely trying to forget his suffering in bouts of drunkenness and debauchery and the ex-peasants assuming more and more the character of townsmen. Such ex-peasants became an increasingly important link between the urban and rural worlds. By the early eighteen-eighties, although educated society still preserved traditional notions about the Russian workman, the Government placed the proletariat among socially dangerous elements.

In 1901, Count Svyatopolk-Mirsky, the Chief of the Gendarmerie, declared of the Russian working man that 'during the last three or four years, from the old good-natured Russian lad there has begun to take shape a peculiar type of semi-literate intellectual who considers it his duty to decry religion and the family, to ignore the law, disobey it and make jokes about it'. This was the type of workman in whom the Marxists often found excellent revolutionary material.

The Russian commercial and industrial middle classes of the late nineteenth century had their own special character. Firstly there were the old-fashioned merchants, an historical Russian estate, without education and of low commercial morality; among these men the customs and outlook of the old Muscovite state were most faithfully preserved, and many of them belonged to the ranks of Old Believers, spiritual descendants of the seventeenth-century schismatic priest Avvakum. Akin to these were the ex-serfs whose forbears, with the connivance of their masters, had become prosperous merchants yet in their family lives still preserved the customs of their original social sphere. Such men, together with the ancestral merchants, were mostly found as barge-owners on the Volga, or as grain-dealers, mill-owners, and textile manufacturers. An outstanding example of an ancestral merchant was the millionaire steamboat-owner of Nizhny Novgorod, the Old Believer Nikolai Bugrov, and of the rich descendant of an ex-serf family, Savva Morozov, the textile tycoon who financed the revolutionaries before 1905 and committed suicide at Vichy in France in May of that year, when the rising was at its height. Such men as Bugrov and Morozov gloried in the power of money, but until the end of the century showed no desire to participate in the social and cultural life of the nation; during the nineties, however, their sons often emerged as modern businessmen, with commercial ideas taken from the West, and joined the advanced literary movements which gained momentum during that decade. These young people would wear fashionable checked suits instead of their elders' traditional caftan. Despite their comparative enlightenment they mostly stayed within their own set, thus tending to perpetuate the traditional isolation of the Russian merchant class from other social spheres.

The second great section of the rising Russian middle classes in the second half of the nineteenth century was composed of the bankers, railway promoters, and heavy industrialists who possessed close ties with the nobility and bureaucracy, held State ranks, and were therefore gentlemen. The political champion of this group was Count Witte. The traditional Russian merchantry had never much concerned themselves about their employees except as tools of profit, and the new industrialists continued to show this long-standing Russian indifference to their workers' welfare, were little interested in technological progress, and until the end of the century formed a close alliance with the bureaucracy with whom they shared the dominant position in the national life. In the countryside the new capitalists clashed at first with the surviving landowning nobility, many of whom had liberal sympathies, and when the nobility through the county councils (*zemstva*) attempted to raise funds by taxing rural industry, the industrialists successfully appealed to the Government to prohibit such activity. In the towns the industrialists gave bribes to the municipal authorities (established as part of the programme of reform in 1870) and countenanced all manner of irregularities in local administration in return for the connivance of the authorities in their exploitation of their workers. The lack of idealism and the commercial opportunism of the employers rebounded on them when the proletarian strike movement began in the nineties and found them illprepared to defend their class interests.

One of the most important consequences of the enactment of the Great Reforms was the considerable expansion of education in Russia. Before the Emancipation the authorities had concerned themselves predominantly with the education of the nobility, one of their principal practical purposes being the provision of recruits for the state service.

The day-to-day functional requirements of the new social order created a demand for greater numbers of trained and semi-trained workers, and the public elementary schools came into existence to provide primary education for such people. During the seventies and eighties there grew up in the countryside, mostly from the ranks of the emancipated peasants, a new kind of semi-professional class—village school-teachers, book-keepers, clerks, assistant doctors —who performed the specialized functions of county council work and who formed an important part of the so-called 'third element' in rural districts, the first two being the landowners and peasants. In the towns increased educational facilities were an important factor in the formation of the improved type of Russian workman already mentioned. As time passed contacts between the new literate classes in town and country grew steadily stronger. Because of their social origins many of these people were radically minded and they constituted an important element of the post-reform intelligentsia.

The term 'intelligentsia' first arose in Russia in the late eighteen-seventies to describe a large heterogeneous social group, radically minded, drawn at one extreme from democratically inclined landowners and governmental officials, and at the other from the higher categories of hired labour. The former constituted the direct link between the pre-reform intelligentsia and their successors. The post-reform intelligentsia, much more numerous and much more varied in composition than their predecessors of earlier decades, were nevertheless profoundly influenced by the cultural and ideological traditions of the latter.

In post-emancipation Russian life the numbers of the intelligentsia far exceeded the demand for their services. The growth of the intelligentsia did not coincide with a rise in the general economic state of the nation, or with an improvement in the cultural level of the masses, and this factor, together with the political stagnation, made large numbers of them superfluous, thus creating a real intellectual proletariat. The Government, although it availed itself of their services where necessary, was hostile to them.

The post-reform Russian intelligentsia suffered keenly as a class from a sense of isolation from the rest of society. Among themselves they underwent a process of severe ideological differentiation, almost fragmentation, but at the same time they strove to assert their identity as a distinct social group. The most powerful factor contributing to their developing sense of community was their keen awareness of their mission, in a society largely indifferent to culture and ideology, as the leaders of the process of enlightenment which, demolishing the survivals of serfdom in the national psychology, was bringing Russia into the family of advanced nations. The combination in the minds of many intellectuals of a feeling of social isolation with a profound sense of mission inspired much of the oppositional tone of Russian literature during the decades preceding the revolution of 1905. This oppositional tone is much stronger and much more sustained than in pre-reform literature.

2

We have seen in the preceding section that the terms of the Emancipation edict bitterly disappointed the peasantry. The radical intelligentsia were no less indignant. Peasant disturbances in the countryside, in the years immediately following 1861, were accompanied by an intense revolutionary ferment in Moscow and St. Petersburg which manifested itself principally in the rise of numerous secret societies. At the same time the bureaucracy took fright at some of the implications of its own reforms and almost immediately re-entered the paths of reaction. The strange result of this was that for twenty years a dual process of

reform and reaction developed; the legal system was re-
formed in 1864 and the system of recruiting in 1874, but
during this decade numerous suspensions or suppressions
of oppositional periodicals took place. The policy of reaction
was a declared policy, championed by the publicist M. N.
Katkov. In 1866 a revolutionary, D. V. Karakozov, acting
as an individual contrary to the wishes of the secret society
to which he belonged, made an unsuccessful attempt upon
the life of Alexander II and was executed. In the same year
the radical periodical, *The Contemporary*, was suppressed.
For two years the intelligentsia, painfully aware of their
incapacity, unaided, to bring about a revolution, languished
without a definite path; but in the magazine *The Week* for
1868/9 there appeared the *Historical Letters* of P. L. Lavrov,
in which the author took up the problem, vital for the post-
Emancipation intelligentsia, of the function of the 'critically
thinking personality' in society. The teaching of the radicals
of the sixties on this issue had been academic: Lavrov
introduces into his views a sharper revolutionary note. 'The
development of the personality in the physical, mental and
moral senses', he wrote, 'the embodiment in social forms
of the ideals of truth and justice—that is the short formula,
as I see it, embracing everything which can be called progress.' Progress of this kind, argued Lavrov, can only be
brought about by a kernel of 'critically thinking personalities'
who are, however, impotent if they attempt to act alone;
their first task must be to introduce critical thought into
the minds of the suffering masses, who will then assist them.
Linked with this teaching there began a crusade of young
Russian intellectuals (some, e.g. P. A. Kropotkin, from the
noblest families) to the people (*khozhdenie v narod*)—a
typically Russian attempt to bring light in a few years into
the darkness of centuries. Their efforts met with little success: the peasants remained apathetic and even hostile.
Nevertheless the Government persecuted them mercilessly,
arrested them in hundreds, and in two great trials, the trial

of the fifty and the trial of the 193 in 1877–78, liquidated their movement. The epic of idealistic Populism was at an end.

After the failure of the crusade to the people, the revolutionaries took fresh thought. The consistently reactionary policy of the Government was provoking profound hostility among broad strata of the population. This hostility reached its peak in 1877 when the Government declared war on Turkey in support of the Southern Slavs—why should a nation risk its sons in a foreign war for liberty if its Government was unwilling to grant liberty at home? The Populists formed a new revolutionary organization, 'Land and Liberty', a member of which, Solovyov (without the consent of the organization), fired unsuccessfully on the Tsar outside the Winter Palace and was executed. In the summer of 1879 'Land and Liberty' split on the issue of whether peaceful propaganda or terrorism was the most effective weapon to bring about the overthrow of Tsarism, and disintegrated into two daughter organizations, 'Black Redistribution' which favoured the first and 'People's Will' which supported the second.

The translation of the first volume of Marx's *Das Kapital* (by Nikolai-on) appeared in Russia in 1872, and, after the disappointment of Populist hopes for a peasant rising, Marxism began to exercise a strong influence upon the minds of disillusioned Populists who were now unsure of their next step. By 1879 certain Populists (for example Plekhanov and Axelrod) were inclining strongly towards Marxism and adhered neither to Black Redistribution nor to People's Will. Thus the whole revolutionary movement was already shaken by severe internal dissensions when on 1 March 1881 the Polish terrorist Grinevich killed Alexander II with a bomb alongside the Catherine Canal in St. Petersburg. When after this outrage the authorities took energetic counter-measures, they found that despite their apparent triumph their enemies had dissolved away as a solid movement of opposition. Populist unity continued to exist in external form for three more years, so long as their magazine *Annals of the Fatherland* was allowed to survive, but in 1884 this organ was suppressed. Thereafter only isolated incidents disturbed the calm which the Government imposed upon society for a decade until the next revolutionary wave began to rise in the mid-nineties. In 1887 a small group of Populists (of whom Lenin's younger brother A. I. Ulyanov was one) were caught conspiring to assassinate the Tsar and executed. In 1891 the Chief of Police in St. Petersburg was assassinated.

The lull in revolutionary activity which marked the years from 1884 to about 1895 had other causes than the ideological splits in the Populist party. With the expansion of the great urban centres and the decline of the countryside the townsman acquired considerably greater importance in the national life, and he rejected with scorn the revolutionary testament of the Populist movement based upon the peasant. Many people, in both town and country, acquiesced in the period of calm partly from fear of governmental punitive measures and partly because they wished to be allowed to live in peace to enjoy the fruits of the new industrial prosperity. The revolutionary movement had thus no longer any broadly based support among the public. The temporary decimation of oppositional thought during these years is reflected in the fact that no single literary organ exists as a rallying point for a unified movement, as *The Contemporary* had been in the sixties and *The Annals of the Fatherland* in the seventies. No all-embracing revolutionary concept united the opponents of Tsarism, and those intellectuals who still felt that something must be done for the people preached in *The Week* the doctrine of 'small deeds', a programme of minor improvements in lower-class life to which the satirist Shchedrin contemptuously referred as a scheme to provide hand-basins and spittoons in the countryside. Other intellectuals became disciples of the teaching of Tolstoy based upon self-perfection and non-resistance to evil as the cornerstones of personal life. This cultivation of personal life, sanctioned by the greatest man of his time, fitted admirably the mood of many thinking people during the eighties, in rebellion against the romantic sacrifice of self to the cause of the revolution which had sustained the members of People's Will. The heroism of the revolutionary for a time was dethroned in the minds of the populace as an ideal and replaced by a creed known as 'the rehabilitation of reality'— the creation of firm foundations for the new post-emancipation social order. Freed from the ideological tyranny of an all-embracing revolutionary creed the individual felt that he now existed as an autonomous personality, valuable in and for himself and not only as a unit of a movement dedicated to social change.

The cult of individualism which gained strength in Russian society in the eighties was nowhere more marked than among the merchants and industrialists who were the leaders of the industrial revolution. The state of social life, in which survivals of serfdom in institutions and in the mentality of the people stood opposed to the mushroom growths of the new order, demanded strong men to carry through the revolution to a successful conclusion despite the overthrow of long-accepted moral standards and the mutilation of human beings which this involved. In industry every man was for himself and the weakest, the workers, went to the wall. The influence of Nietzsche, whose works appeared in translation in 1892, came to reinforce the cult of individualism everywhere.

The first signs of a change in social mood in Russia after the lull in revolutionary activity of the late eighties belong to the years 1891/2. During these years a great famine and a widespread cholera epidemic caused grievous suffering. These disasters were seriously mismanaged by the authorities and a great wave of unrest and resentment spread through the peasantry and the lower urban classes. There were still, however, no clear signs of the existence of a unified revolutionary movement among the intelligentsia capable of turning muffled discontent into organized opposition to bureaucratic Tsarism. When Alexander III died in 1894 there seemed little reason to doubt his expressed conviction that the Russian monarchy was the strongest in the world.

In 1883 Plekhanov founded abroad the Emancipation of Labour party, the first Russian Marxist organization. In his two books, *Socialism and the Political Struggle* (1883) and *Our Disagreements* (1885), he analysed the reasons for the failure of the Populist movement. In 1885 together with other *émigrés* he published *A Projected Programme for a Russian Workmen's Socialist Democratic Party*. In his writings Plekhanov looked at the contemporary state of Russian society in which the rapid growth of an industrial proletariat which included large numbers of ex-peasants was accompanied by the development of a commercial and industrial *bourgeoisie* which in their persistent efforts to extend their rights often came into conflict with the old landed gentry. This state of affairs, argued Plekhanov, presaged the eventual absorption of the great majority of the peasantry by urban industry (they would be 'boiled down in the cauldron of capitalism') and the passage of all landed property into the possession of big holders. Populist dreams of the non-capitalistic evolution of Russia were nonsense. The *mir* and the *artel*, collectivistic psychology and all that the Populists described as 'socialistic tendencies' were 'relics of an outworn economic system' and would inevitably disintegrate under the impact of advancing capitalism. It was foolish to attempt to obstruct the development of capitalism in Russia because such development was historically inevitable, just as the eventual socialistic transformation of society from capitalism was inevitable. It was the task of revolutionary intellectuals to strive to further the progress of capitalism in Russia and thus lend impetus to the unfolding of the already determined course of history. The doctrine of the decisive role of the individual in the formation of history was an idealistic illusion.

Between 1885 and 1895, as Russian Marxism gained strength and coherence as a movement, idealistic Populism was supplanted by 'critical' Populism championed by Nikolai Mikhailovsky. Mikhailovsky's chief sociological works were *What is Progress* (1869), *The Struggle for Individuality* (1875–6), and *Heroes and the Mob* (1882). The teaching expounded in these works was based upon the author's conviction that the supreme value in human evolution, which had affirmed itself above all errors and passions, was human individuality. It was the task of mankind to create a social system in which the interests of society would be reconciled with the harmonious development of the individual. This harmonious development was prevented in a modern capitalistic society by the division of labour, technological advance, and fierce economic competition which, all acting together, made the individual an insignificant cog in the social machine. True respect for the individual could only be found in a new order based upon socialism which proclaims the solidarity of all who labour. The individual would eventually be emancipated by labour. Socialism meant the emancipation of the people—the majority of individuals—through labour.

The 'critical' side of Mikhailovsky's Populism was based upon the bitter experience of the Populists of the seventies who, seeking in the people allies in their battle to create a social order in Russia based upon the ideals of truth and justice, found them apathetic, superstitious, and benighted. Mikhailovsky insisted that it was the intellectuals' duty to work for the emancipation of the people through the establishment of socialism, but they must not blind themselves to the people's imperfections (not altogether their fault), and in their revolutionary aspirations they must remain faithful to their own ideals and constantly strive to imbue the masses with respect for these ideals.

Mikhailovsky rejected the Marxist theory of the universal pattern of social evolution, according to which the differences between the state of Russian and Western societies were due to the gradation of the same historical process. In his view each national society developed according to its own characteristics. Plekhanov regarded only the proletariat everywhere as a truly revolutionary class. Mikhailovsky believed that Russia's revolution would come about through an alliance between the peasants, the proletariat, and the intellectuals.

During the nineties for the first time in Russian social life two conflicting trends contended for the loyalty of the revolutionary intelligentsia—'critical' Populism and Marxism. From about 1895, unhindered by the authorities, the two sides waged open polemical warfare around the old issue of the path of Russia's future development. Marxist propagandists went to work among the proletariat in the large cities, offering them not the incomprehensible theories of earlier revolutionaries but active help to fight their grievances of long hours, managerial fines, and brutal foremen. These propagandists made every effort to persuade the workers to draw political conclusions from their economic grievances. In 1896 and 1897 great strikes took place in the cotton-mills of St. Petersburg, and it was during these strikes that workmen were addressed and organized for the first time by Marxists. These events marked the real beginning of the organized working-class movement in Russia, and by the way in which the strikers behaved society was obliged to revise its traditional notion of the Russian working man. In February 1898 a congress of Marxist groups was held in Minsk at which it was decided to form a Social Democrat Workers' Party, and although the leaders of the newly formed party were arrested immediately after the congress, the functions of leadership were assumed by 'The

League of Social Democrats Abroad', centred in Switzerland. In 1903, after four years of industrial recession, great strikes took place, starting at Rostov and spreading over southern Russia from Odessa to Baku, and during these strikes the Social Democrats became recognized as the leaders of the working-class movement. In the summer of 1903 the party held its second congress, first in Brussels and then in London; at this congress dissension over the nature and organization of the party and over the composition of the editorial board of their newspaper *The Spark* brought about their cleavage into Bolsheviks (Majoritarians—led by Lenin) whose views prevailed, and Mensheviks (Minoritarians).

Whereas the Marxists were predominantly the party of the working class, the Social Revolutionary party, which sprang from the Populist movement, enjoyed the largest measure of support that the Russian people in general was capable of extending to any politically active group. The decision to form the party was taken in 1900 at a secret meeting held in Kharkov; and in 1902 representatives of Social Revolutionary groups inside Russia met exiles in Switzerland and agreed to form with them a single unified organization. In the same year the newly formed party created as part of their machinery a combat organization with the task of performing assassinations. In April 1902 Stepan Balmashev assassinated the Minister of the Interior, Sipyagin, in July 1904 Sipyagin's successor Von Pleve was assassinated by Yegor Sazonov, and in February 1905 the Grand Duke Sergei by Ivan Kalyaev. The Marxists disapproved of such violence because they regarded it as their task to destroy classes and not individuals.

Although the nineties were marked by diverse oppositional trends to Tsarism (Liberalism also played its part), the revolution of 1905 was a national mutiny against a Government which through its ill-conceived counter-measures against revolutionary groups succeeded in alienating the sympathy of almost the entire population. Of the Tsar's manifesto of 17 October granting a constitution it can be said, as of few events in history, that it truly represented the will of the people.

1. IDEAS AND OUTLOOK

MAXIM GORKY was the pen-name of Alexei Maximovich Peshkov, who was born on 16 (28) March 1868 in Nizhny Novgorod (in 1932 renamed Gorky) and died on 18 June 1936 in Moscow. His first story, 'Makar Chudra', was published in the Tiflis newspaper *The Caucasus* for 12 September 1892. At this time it was the custom in Russian provincial journalism for new contributors to sign their work either with their initials or with a pseudonym. On the spur of the moment, sitting in the editor's office, Peshkov decided to sign himself 'M. Gorky', and this spontaneously invented pseudonym turned out to be particularly suitable for the young writer because the word 'gorky' combined the two meaning of 'wretched', relating to the harsh conditions of his life in boyhood and youth, and 'bitter', describing the flavour of his work for the Russian reading public of the eighteen-nineties. He brought them a bitter reminder that while many of them concerned themselves with aesthetic problems, in the manner of the new poetic school, or with Tolstoyan meditation upon questions of personal morality, millions of their wretched countrymen were living, as he had lived, in conditions of intolerable filth, poverty, and ignorance.

Gorky's father, Maxim Savvatievich Peshkov, died on 29 July 1871 in Astrakhan, of cholera contracted from his three-year-old son, who was also seriously ill but recovered. His mother, *née* Varvara Vasilievna Kashirina, died in her father's house in Nizhny Novgorod on 5 August 1879 of galloping consumption. During the intervening eight years

Gorky lived in Nizhny with his maternal grandparents, Vasili Vasilievich and Akulina Ivanovna Kashirin (*née* Muratova), the owners of a small dyeing business. During this time he rarely saw his mother, who hated her father's house and paid only fleeting visits to it; on the few occasions when they met, she treated him with reserve because she blamed him for her husband's premature death. Gorky was thus, to all intents and purposes, a complete orphan in childhood. At this time he first experienced the agonizing loneliness from which he suffered in varying degrees of intensity throughout his boyhood and youth and which persistently recurs in his fictional characters as the source of their bitterest unhappiness.

The central figures of Gorky's childhood were his maternal grandparents. Through them he made his first acquaintance with the idea of God. Vasili Kashirin spoke of God to his grandson as 'a sword over the earth, the scourge of sinners'. For him religion was a system of mechanical devotion, devoid of love or charity; he prayed by rote, terrified of divine retribution if he should omit a single word, even a mere syllable, from time-honoured forms. In the traditional manner of the Russian merchant class Kashirin called upon the despotic authority of his God of fear to support his tyrannical attitude to the younger members of his family. Out of Gorky's childish awe of his grandfather's avenging deity grew in large part his later hostility to all organized religion, which he saw as the prop of oppressive governments. But this hostility had other roots. For his grandmother, Akulina Ivanovna, the Christian faith meant not punishment for failure to observe rigid rules and ritual but readiness to accept the inevitable hardships of life, together with profound compassion for all who suffered them. During his childhood, because of his great love for his grandmother, Gorky was greatly influenced by her view of endurance and compassion as the cardinal Christian virtues. When he left home, however, and began to formulate his opinions from his own experience, he found that he was temperamentally incapable of pitying people who suffered if they accepted their bitter lot too passively and made no attempt to change it. He came to regard the too willing endurance of unnecessary hardships as an historical psychological vice of the Russian people encouraged by their Church. He saw the compliant victims of tyranny and injustice as just as much to blame for their suffering as their oppressors. During his boyhood and youth Gorky experienced in his own person almost every kind of suffering known to the most wretched of his compatriots; yet, through the exercise of the virtues of resilience and pugnacity, reinforced by the blessing of a robust constitution, he did not succumb, but emerged from his ordeal spiritually enriched. He looked for the same virtues in others, and their absence in so many of his friends and acquaintances often transformed his spontaneous sympathy for them, as under-dogs, into something resembling contempt.

Gorky's increasing antipathy, as he grew older, to many aspects of official Christian teaching in Russia, because of what he considered to be their harmful influence upon the national psychology, does not alter the fact that the cast of his mind was essentially religious, in the sense that he could not live without an idea of God as a spiritual ideal to which to aspire. As we shall see, this deep-rooted religiosity was one of the principal reasons for his repeated disputes with Lenin.

2

Defiant pugnacity was one of the most characteristic traits of Gorky's nature and he expressed it from his earliest years in chivalrous if sometimes imprudent acts of vengeance against tyrants. Once, for example, when his stepfather, Evgeni Maximov, kicked his pregnant mother in the stomach, he flew at him with a carving knife in his hand. Later, when a group of peasants (in the village of Kandy-

bovo, Kherson province) were flogging a woman for
marital infidelity, he attempted to rescue her and was himself assaulted and left for dead. These were both the actions
of a person gallant by nature and particularly resentful of
attacks upon women. Gorky's rebellious spirit did not always, however, assert itself so chivalrously. During the
winters of 1880–1 and 1881–2 and from April 1883 to
August 1884, he lived in the household of his grandmother's sister, Matryona Sergeeva, consisting apart from
Matryona of her two sons, Valentin and Viktor, and Valentin's wife. This family filled him with fear and despair
because not only did they worship the same God of vengeance as old Kashirin but, thanks to the successful commercial activity of the elder brother Valentin, they enjoyed
an apparently soundly-based and durable prosperity which
made them self-satisfied and censorious. Gorky was more
deeply offended by the Sergeevs' self-righteous gentility
than by the brutality and violence which he saw among the
Kashirins, but whereas among the latter he could relieve
his feelings by meeting violence with violence, with his
middle-class relatives he found no excuse for physical
assault and could only nurse impotent rage. In a person of
his pugnacious temperament, however, suppressed resentment demanded an outlet; and we find him venting his
hatred of his surroundings in acts of pointless mischief such
as stopping the clocks by blowing dust into them or making
the chimneys smoke by stuffing them with paper.

Although Gorky was only a boy when he lived with the
Sergeevs, his actions of domestic sabotage in their household were characteristic of a certain type of aggressive
Russian rebelliousness which was a feature of the national
character fundamental enough to have found embodiment
in a famous hero of Russian folk poetry, Vasili Buslaev, the
tempestuous burgher of Novgorod the Great. This quality
is described in Russian by the untranslatable word
'ozorstvo', the meaning of which is best illustrated by

Buslaev's behaviour as the folk epic describes it. Buslaev hated the commercial way of life of his fellow-burghers (just as Gorky hated that of his prosperous relatives), but he could find no better way of expressing his hatred than by provoking street brawls with the assistance of a picked gang of accomplices, and, later in life, indulging in piracy on the Volga—activities which, like Gorky's boyish pranks, did no one any good, but relieved the feelings of their perpetrator. Gorky, indeed, felt the presence of a kindred spirit in Vasili Buslaev and in 1897 he began a play about him, but did not get further than his hero's boastful opening monologue in which, having beautified the earth, he holds it up to God, exclaiming, 'You launched it into space as a rock but I have turned it into a precious emerald.' This combination of impudent lack of respect for authority and a passionate desire to improve life around him is characteristic of the Russian *ozornik*, a national type of which both Gorky and Tolstoy, in their own ways, were good examples. When they met, each recognized the type in the other. In a different field of activity Bakunin may be cited as an example of the same type.

It is interesting that in February 1898, when the publisher S. P. Dorovatovsky asked him to write an introduction to the collection of his stories and sketches which was about to appear, Gorky, after some delay, replied: 'I am annoyed that I cannot write a preface but I find it really impossible. I have tried but everything comes out just as if I were squaring up to someone and challenging him to a fight, or as if I had sinned and were tearfully repentant.' These words are strongly reminiscent of those in which in *My Apprenticeship* Gorky describes one of the two beings who, he says, lived within him as a fifteen year old boy:

. . . he realised that life's frightful humdrum exerted a ruthless power which might easily lop off his head or crush him under a dirty heel. And so he summoned every atom of his strength in self-defence, baring his teeth, clenching his fists, always ready for a fight or an argument. His feelings of love and compassion found expression in action and, as became the gallant hero of a French novel, he would bare his sword and strike an aggressive pose at the slightest provocation.

The truculent urchin from the back streets of Nizhny Novgorod reasserted himself in the well-known writer. Throughout his career Gorky continuously returned in his fictional characters to this pugnacious, chivalrous, destructive individual whom he rather admired in himself. We have the hero of his story 'A saucy fellow' (1896), the compositor Nikolai Gvozdev who deliberately changes the text of a leading article in his newspaper because he is disgusted by the gulf between the editor's fine words and the unjust manner in which he treats his subordinates; we have Ilya Lunev, the ambitious hero of the novel *The Three of Them* (1901) and Foma Gordeev, the rebellious merchant's son (1899), Yegor Bulychov (1933) the self-made industrialist whose business is swept away by the Bolshevik seizure of power and (in *Klim Samgin* (1927–36)) the Dostoevskian 'repentant millionaire' Lyutov who commits suicide out of a sense of offence at life's injustices. Gorky shows considerable sympathy for each one of these characters.

Another person, Gorky tells us in *My Apprenticeship*, lived in him at the age of fifteen by the side of the irrepressible fighter for justice:

. . . having seen too much filth and loathsomeness this person had lost heart. Life's frightful humdrum had made him sceptical and suspicious and he looked with helpless compassion upon everyone including himself. He longed to lead a quiet retired life far away from towns and people. He dreamed of going to Persia, of entering a monastery, of living in a forester's hut or in a railway guard's cabin, or of becoming a night watchman somewhere on the outskirts of a city. The fewer people, the more remote, the better.

The most typical deed of this frightened person during Gorky's formative years is of course his attempt to commit suicide in December 1887. This was a confession of complete defeat by life. A second characteristic action is his endeavour in 1889 to obtain from Tolstoy a piece of land on which to establish a quiet secluded agricultural colony where he could find refuge from the mental turmoil which continued to torment him for five years after his attempted suicide (after 1892 the act of creative writing brought him relief). In his fictional world Gorky returns as often to the figure of the frightened boy as to that of the saucy rebel, but his attitude to such characters is not always favourable: he shows affectionate compassion towards the mute, brow-beaten Pavel Gibly in *Paul the Wretched* and towards the timid dreamer Yakov Filimonov in *The Three of Them*, but in *The Life of an Unnecessary Man* (1908) the cowardly sneak Evsei Klimkov grows up to become a police spy and Klim Samgin, pathetically anxious in youth to win everyone's approval, is presented in manhood as a typical liberal intellectual (as Gorky saw such people) concerned only with his own well-being and safety and afraid to commit himself to struggle for the welfare of all mankind. Throughout his life Gorky betrayed a petty *bourgeois* hankering after comfort and a peaceful existence which was probably the result of his youthful suffering; his other self, the fighter, disapproved of this weakness and his merciless scourging of Samgin is partly inspired by this disapproval. The Russian word 'sam' means 'self'.

3

Of the five official estates of Tsarist Russian society Gorky during his formative years saw very little of the nobility or clergy, and neither plays a significant part in his literary work. His knowledge of the peasantry in youth was acquired for the most part during a sojourn of three months in the village of Krasnovidovo, near Kazan, in the year 1888. His experience in this village (he was fortunate to escape being burned to death) strengthened the inborn contempt and

distrust which as a townsman he felt for country dwellers.
He concluded on the spot that the fundamental characteristics of the Russian peasant were greed, cunning,
drunkenness, respect for force, and a particularly repellent
love of cruelty for its own sake, practised as the art of dis-
covering by deliberate experiment how much physical pain
a human being can endure. This remained essentially his
view throughout his life. He saw in peasant psychology
some of the most tenacious survivals of what he described
as the 'second soul' of the Russian people—Asiatic modes
of behaviour and patterns of thought which recalled the
long Tartar yoke, and which the passage of centuries did
not change. In his essay 'On the Russian peasantry', published in Berlin in 1922, he describes how a seventeenth-
century chronicler related that the peasants in his time
stuffed gunpowder into men's mouths and then blew them
up, and he continues: 'In 1918 and 1919, Russian peasants
did exactly the same thing in the Don country and in the
Ukraine. They stuffed men with dynamite cartridges.' This
essay is omitted from the thirty-volume edition of Gorky's
works, as is his article on a related theme, 'Two Souls',
which he published in December 1915 in his monthly magazine, *Chronicles*; the Soviet authorities, striving all the time
to reconcile conflicts between town and country, do not
take kindly to the fact that their literary idol so feared and
distrusted the peasantry.

Gorky was himself by origin a petty *bourgeois* (*meshchanin*)
and he knew this class of society intimately. He first
discerned their predominant vices—envy, malice, self-
righteousness, intellectual and spiritual torpor—among his
relatives, the Sergeevs (see page 25) because the Kashirins,
although in their best days very prosperous, never lost the
ignorance, brutality, and barbaric customs typical of their
original way of life as serfs. In the publicist writings of the
first decade of his literary career, Gorky chose as the target
of his bitterest attacks the figure of the *meshchanin*. As well

as possessing the literal meaning of 'petty bourgeois', this word may also be translated figuratively as 'philistine', in which sense it refers to individuals of any social class who show the vices Gorky detested in the Sergeevs. During the eighteen-nineties Gorky broadened and deepened his concept of the *meshchanin* and the outlook which distinguished him as a social type—*meshchanstvo*—'petty bourgeois mentality' and he came to see as an important factor in the spread of this mentality in Russian society the moral and religious teaching of Tolstoy and Dostoevsky. Throughout his life this linking of the names of Russia's two greatest novelists with an outlook which both abominated remained one of the most striking facets of his thought (see page 37.)

The first thirty years of Maxim Gorky's life were spent almost in their entirety in and about the principal towns of the region of the middle and lower Volga—Nizhny Novgorod, Saratov, Kazan. The local heroes of this region were its merchants, men whose businesses and personal fortunes were based upon the strength of the mighty river. Such men were usually of one of two types: ancestral merchants of low commercial morality preserving in their outlook many of the prejudices and superstitions of pre-Petrine Russia; or ex-serfs who during the nineteenth century, with the connivance of their masters, had become prosperous business men, yet, like the Kashirins, still preserved in their family lives the customs of their original social sphere. These merchants were found for the most part as barge-owners, grain-dealers, mill-owners, or textile-manufacturers. Their fellow townsmen admired them greatly, referred to them as their 'iron men', and regarded them as their greatest claim to glory in the eyes of the outside world. Gorky, for his part, although he deplored the ruthlessness and dishonesty with which they conducted their affairs, saw in them an active and dynamic element standing apart from the stagnant and apathetic way of life of the great majority of his regional compatriots. He was fascinated not only by their virtues of energy, enterprise, and resolution, but also by their love of life, their contempt for the conventional morality of the petty *bourgeoisie*, and their equal readiness to spend as well as to make money. Sometimes—he tells us in his memoirs—after long years of hard work and slave-like devotion to their businesses, some of these men would rebel against the constricting ties of affairs and family, throw everything up and go off somewhere. When they did so, he relates, stories of their boisterous exploits made the 'superfluous men' of the nobility and Dostoevsky's 'underground man' seem like 'dwarfs walking upon the stilts of fine words'. There is no doubt that Gorky's attitude to these men was tinged by local patriotism, but they were indeed a colourful social group, and they attracted the attention of other writers besides him, notably Leskov. Their weakness as a social force lay in the fact that many of them did not subject their boundless energy to the control of disciplined thought. Gorky was painfully aware in their erratic careers of what he considered to be one of the fundamental spiritual tragedies of Russian life—the divorce of the principle of will from that of reason.

During his sojourn in Kazan, from the year 1884 to 1888, described in *My Universities*, Gorky became closely acquainted with yet another social group—the revolutionary intelligentsia still predominantly Populist by persuasion. He quickly realized that they were exceptional in contemporary Russian society because they were deeply concerned about issues greater than their personal comfort—the welfare of the Russian people and the future of Russia were their constant preoccupations. Gorky saw in these men the natural allies of the downtrodden masses, among whom he had spent his earlier years, in their struggle against bureaucratic capitalism for their elementary human rights. At the same time, however, he was painfully aware that these natural allies were estranged from each other by an unbridgeable gulf of misunderstanding caused by centuries of class isolation in Russian life. The people regarded the intelligentsia as noblemen whose interests must inevitably clash with their own; the Populists, for their part, thought of the people as the embodiment of wisdom, goodness, and spiritual beauty, and they had been bitterly disillusioned when they made direct contact with them in the eighteen-seventies and found them to be ignorant, brutal, and superstitious.

The abyss of hostility and misunderstanding which divided the Russian people and intelligentsia in the nineteenth century played an important part in Gorky's personal life during the four years he spent in Kazan. Gorky belonged to the people through his harsh experience of life but to the intelligentsia through his passionate love for books and his burning desire to change the social order in Russia. Combining in himself elements of both classes, he longed to see their knowledge and understanding of each other improved, and he dreamed of the day when the ideals of the one would be united with the discontent and elemental strength of the other in an unconquerable alliance against Tsarist tyranny and injustice. Youthfully confident in Kazan in his ability to perform tremendous tasks, he conceived there the heroic plan of reconciling in his own person the two estranged worlds. Thus as a worker he toiled twelve hours a day in a grocery shop the profits from which were added to the revolutionaries' meagre financial resources; as revolutionary intellectual he strove to enlighten the people by repeating to the workers with whom he spent the days the radical ideas he heard from the thinkers in the evenings. For a short while he deluded himself into believing that as a reconciler of historical differences between workers and intellectuals he had found a mission in life which only a person of his unique combination of talents and experience could perform. This delusion, however, was quickly demolished by reality. He found that the radicals plundered the grocery shop till for their personal needs; and that the workers thought it good fun to set on the radicals with iron weights. He bitterly realized that he was personally powerless to bring about an alliance between the two, even within the confines of a single Russian town like Kazan. This disillusionment robbed him of his desperately desired sense of purpose in life; and his inability to feel at one with either the workers or the intellectuals made him feel agonizingly lonely. This feeling was intensified by the deaths of his grandmother and grandfather in February and May 1887. In December, bewildered and pathless in the present, without hope for the future, he made a determined attempt to end his own life.

Despite his bitter disappointment in Kazan, Gorky remained faithful throughout his life to his youthful vision of a revolutionary alliance between the workers and the radical intelligentsia as the surest foundation of a new social order. His untiring personal efforts, between 1906 (after the failure of the first revolution) and his death in 1936, to improve the educational level of the Russian proletariat were inspired and sustained by his conviction that the existence of an *élite* among the working class would accelerate the implementation of such an alliance. When the revolution finally succeeded in 1917 he was terrified lest Lenin should use the still small group of educated Russian workers as an instrument to assist him in establishing autocratic control over the peasantry, and in so doing condemn them to certain destruction at the hands of a barbaric mob. This fear inspired many of the polemical articles he published in his newspaper *New Life* after the seizure of power by the Bolsheviks. Gorky first gave artistic expression to his respect for the revolutionary intellectual, and his distrust of the mob for whom the thinker sacrifices himself, in the legend of Danko related in the story 'Old Izergil' (1894). In his romantic mood of the early eighteen-nineties he exalts the selflessness of a leader who gives his life for his people; faced with the realities of the aftermath of revolution in 1918 he realized that the wholesale sacrifice of the best sons of the Russian nation might well bring it to disaster.

Gorky's youthful experience brought him into close contact with one more group of Russian people who, like the merchantry and the intelligentsia, both pleased and displeased him. These were the down-and-outs, the flotsam and jetsam of the new industrial society, the human wastage of the rapidly disintegrating patriarchal order. The down-and-outs resembled the radical intelligentsia in that they consisted of recruits from all the established social estates but, as a group, possessed distinctive characteristics of outlook which set them apart from the rest of the population. Among them Gorky discerned with approval 'an attitude of derisive hostility towards everything on earth and of couldn't care less towards themselves'. 'All of them [he writes] were people who had broken out of the main stream of life, but they seemed to have created a life of their own, gay and independent of others.' The two extremes of the intelligentsia's profound concern about every facet of Russian life and the down-and-outs' cynical indifference to everything, were poles of outlook between which in his early manhood Gorky himself fluctuated violently according to his changing moods. As his mood swung from one extreme to the other he felt drawn now to the intelligentsia, now to the down-and-outs, yet he was prevented from throwing in his lot with either through a persistent feeling that neither represented a truly positive social force. The down-and-outs had no constructive ability to place alongside the intelligentsia's reasoning power, but the latter squandered this power in futile theorizing and showed exaggerated respect for book knowledge. These were the reasons, Gorky concluded, for the feelings of defeat and frustration which he found to be widespread among them.

4

In an allegorical sketch entitled 'Of the Siskin who lied and the Woodpecker who loved the truth', published in the

Samara newspaper *The Volga Messenger* for 4 September 1893, Gorky first broached a problem which was to pre-occupy him throughout the first period of his literary career —the problem of the nature of truth. In a later sketch entitled 'More of the devil', published in the Marxist maga-zine *Life* for February 1899, he wrote: 'There is one kind of truth which is necessary to Mankind for, with the fire of shame, it burns from their hearts all forms of filth and triviality; but another kind which falls like a stone upon their heads and destroys within them all desire to live— and they perish.' In the early sketch the Siskin is the bearer of the first truth, and the Woodpecker proclaims the second. With other birds they inhabit a certain grove. Of all the birds in this grove the crows sing the loudest and, in their song, lament that Fate treats them unkindly, but in the prevailing circumstances of life they see no alternative but to submit to its blows. The nightingales warble their agree-ment with the crows. Horrified by such defeatism, the small waxen-beaked Siskin, the humblest bird in the grove, summons all the other birds to leave their comfortable nests and fly away, to create, elsewhere, a way of life in-formed by a more heroic spirit. The birds are impressed by the Siskin's call, but, before they finally resolve to obey it, the voice of the industrious Woodpecker is heard, restraining them, warning them that outside the grove lies danger, and demanding from the Siskin proof that a more heroic life is possible. The Siskin weeps and confesses that he has no such proof. The birds return to their perches, grateful to the Woodpecker for his warning.

The meaning of this allegory is that the Woodpecker has on his side the truth of fact but the Siskin proclaims the truth of the spirit. The grove is a symbolical representation of contemporary Russia. In the small, rebellious Siskin Gorky presents himself, an unknown provincial journalist. The figure of the Woodpecker, endlessly tapping at the tree, is a symbol of the small businessman, eternally preoccupied with his own trivial affairs, a type who was coming to the fore in Russian society of the eighteen-eighties and early nineties. The crows echo the despondent mood of many members of the intelligentsia at the time. The sweet song of the nightingales is the voice of the poets and critics who were reaffirming Pushkin's belief in the supremacy of the artist among men and in beauty as the greatest artistic virtue. In Gorky's view mercantile opportunism intellectual defeatism, and aestheticism were the mortal sins of Russian society when he wrote his allegory. Forgetting the plight of the people, business men thought only of making enormous profits; the intelligentsia occupied themselves with self-perfection and maintained a prudent silence about social issues, and the poets were absorbed by self-adulation and formal experimentation. Gorky, of course, was alarmed by this desertion of the revolutionary cause by some of the best men in Russian society, but he was even more alarmed by his suspicion that these men's preoccupation with private material interests and with trivial problems of personal life was a sign that they were allowing their moral values to be undermined by their surroundings. Always convinced that a sound personality was based upon sound moral values he feared that he was seeing in Russia the beginnings of the distortion of the human personality by capitalism, a process which he thought was already far advanced in the West. It was this fear which inspired him to write much of his early publicist work, including his allegory of the Siskin and the Woodpecker. The truth of fact in contemporary Russia, as Gorky saw it, consisted of a base social milieu which was exercising a corruptive influence upon the ethical standards of even the most cultured people; the truth of the spirit, in his view, demanded that these people should not only resist moral contamination by their surroundings but should struggle to transform these surroundings before they were finally irredeemably debased by them.

5

Gorky's concern for the fate of the human personality in a once patriarchal society, rapidly becoming commercialized, is fully expressed in two long articles, 'Notes on the petty bourgeois mentality' (1905) and 'The destruction of personality' (1908). In these articles Gorky deplores the fact that human beings, once heroic, have, in the nineteenth and twentieth centuries, taken on the pigmy personality of the 'petty bourgeois'. The basis of petty bourgeois personality in Gorky's view is self-centred individualism expressed in the pursuit of private property; with this he contrasts heroic individualism, the distinguishing characteristic of the true leader of men who scorns personal aggrandizement and devotes himself wholly to the furtherance of the well-being of his fellow creatures. Two principal tasks face such a leader in the modern world, the subjugation of the forces of nature to human control and the bringing together of all mankind into a single fraternal union; he will succeed in these tasks through the exercise of the greatest of all human qualities—reasoning power.

The petty bourgeois, in Gorky's view, is incapable of devoting his reasoning power to the welfare of all mankind because he is wholly absorbed in the pursuit of his private material interests; his particular kind of individualism sets one man against another instead of reconciling them; his loftiest ideological concept is a stable social order which will give him every opportunity to enjoy in peace the benefits of his private property acquired in bitter competition with other petty bourgeois; when his comfort and security are threatened he is tempted to resort to violence and hooliganism in their defence.

Gorky's views on the nature of the petty bourgeois as summarized above contain nothing basically original. He provoked lively debate among his contemporaries, however, through linking his hatred for the petty bourgeois mentality with his temperamental antipathy to the widespread influence of the religious and moral teaching of Tolstoy and Dostoevsky among the Russian intelligentsia at the end of the nineteenth and beginning of the twentieth century. In the first part of *The Life of Klim Samgin* Gorky writes:

A writer of the greatest genius, so keenly sensitive to the force of evil, that he seemed to have created it, to be the Devil unmasking himself—this artist, in a country where the majority of masters were slaves like their servants, cried hysterically: Humble thyself proud man. Endure, proud man.

And his voice was echoed, no less loudly, by that of another genius, powerfully and insistently proclaiming that only one path leads to freedom—the path of non-resistance to evil.

Gorky was intensely proud of Tolstoy's artistic genius, firstly out of Russian patriotism and secondly because such greatness was in his eyes a token of the heights of achievement of which human beings were capable—a challenge to Christian teaching which asserted that men could not manage their earthly affairs without the help of a supernatural Deity. At the same time, however, Gorky abhorred the personal religion which Tolstoy evolved after his spiritual crisis of the seventies, in particular his insistence that one should not resist evil by force, and his call to his fellow-Russians to perfect and simplify themselves. This teaching, in Gorky's view, could only produce in its followers a passive attitude to life, because non-resistance to evil meant tolerance of the evils of Tsarist society, and self-simplification meant trivial and futile preoccupation with personal life, a shameful pursuit among cultured men in a country like Russia where the common people were so desperately in need of education—'they still use the wooden plough, fear sorcerers and believe in devils'. In his sketch 'More of the devil' (1899) Gorky depicts a typical Tolstoyan intellectual, Ivan Ivanovich Ivanov, who, seeking spiritual perfection, begs the devil to help him to tear all passion from his heart; at Ivanov's request the devil leaves him capable of experiencing no other emotion but compassion, then looks at him with astonishment: 'He seemed somehow to sag, to loll forward as though all his bones had been extracted. He sat open-mouthed in his chair and his face shone with that indescribable ecstasy which is most characteristic of congenital idiots.' Among the characters of Tolstoy's fictional world Gorky especially disliked the figure of the fatalistic peasant Platon Karataev in *War and Peace*, and he applied to the cult of Tolstoyanism among the Russian intelligentsia the contemptuous epithet 'Karataevism', meaning a passive and anarchical attitude to life. Implicit in this term was a condemnation of Tolstoy's rejection of knowledge and reason, as effective instruments to help him to find solutions to his spiritual problems, in favour of natural peasant wisdom. Gorky the erstwhile slum-dweller's acquisition of knowledge had been too painful a process for him to regard with favour the aristocrat's scorn for the culture which he had known since birth, and his unhappy experience of rustic life in the village of Krasnovidovo was unlikely to make him sympathize with Tolstoy's idealization of the peasant.

The virulence of Gorky's antipathy to Tolstoy's social teaching varied according to the Russian social climate. His sharp criticisms in 1905 belong to the rising tide of hostility to Tsarism which embraced all social classes and culminated in the revolution of that year; in 1908, when the feeling of political despair which seized the intelligentsia after the failure of the revolution was at its height, Gorky refused to play any part in the celebration in honour of Tolstoy's eightieth birthday, declaring that although the great writer filled him with admiration he nevertheless also repelled him; but in 1918–19, after the successful revolution, he wrote and published his famous reminiscences of Tolstoy, in which he does not conceal his reverence for his 'God-like' subject.

Gorky's abhorrence of Dostoevsky's moral and religious teaching was equalled only by the fascinated interest with which he returned again and again to his work. 'The more I study him', he wrote in a letter to the critic Ivanov-Razumnik on 29 October 1913, 'the more he rouses my indignation.' The enormous influence of Dostoevsky's religious seeking, and of his preoccupation with the forces of evil, upon the outlook of the Russian intelligentsia during the years of successful Governmental reaction from 1906 to 1912 was in Gorky's view one of the most repellent aspects of the morbid psychological state of Russian society during those years. In October 1910 in response to the prevailing public interest in Dostoevsky the Moscow Arts Theatre produced an experimental adaptation of *The Brothers Karamazov*. In July 1913, while living in Rimini, Gorky heard that they further proposed to put on a dramatization of the violently anti-socialist novel *The Possessed* under the title 'Nikolai Stavrogin'. This proposal infuriated him, and towards the end of August he wrote an article entitled 'On Karamazovism' and sent it to the editor of the newspaper *The Russian Word*, where it appeared on 22 September. It was accompanied in this newspaper by a statement from the author defining his purpose in writing it: 'I am firmly convinced that preaching Dostoevsky's diseased ideas from the stage can only unsettle still more the already shattered nerves of society.' The article was widely read and from 23 September, daily, the Russian press carried items under headings such as 'Gorky versus Dostoevsky', 'Gorky accuses Dostoevsky'. Conservative critics joined the fray, accusing Gorky of wishing to suppress the presentation of ideas for no other reason than that he disagreed with them. Finally on 27 October Gorky sent an open letter to *The Russian Word* under the title 'More on Karamazovism' in which he fiercely attacked the Dostoevskian notion of 'ultimate freedom', declaring that this notion in Russia had always concealed an urge away from action towards contemplation, away from culture towards savagery and barbarism.

The burden of Gorky's spiritual hostility to Dostoevsky's

favourite ideas is contained in the article 'On Karamazov-ism'. Here he writes:

> Incontestably, undoubtedly, Dostoevsky is a genius, but he is our evil genius. With astonishing profoundity he felt, understood and delightedly portrayed two illnesses fostered in Russian people by their ugly history and their harsh, painful existence; the sadistic cruelty of the totally disillusioned nihilist and—its opposite—the masochism of the downtrodden, bewildered creature capable not only of enjoying his suffering but even of finding malicious pleasure in parading this suffering before everyone including himself. Having been mercilessly beaten, he boasts about it.

Gorky's antipathy to Dostoevsky's gospel of endurance may be linked with his rejection, after he left his grand-parents' home, of his beloved grandmother's religion of uncomplaining acceptance. He tells us in the story 'Twenty-six men and a girl' that he had known many Russian people who seemed to be proud of their suffering because it was the only experience through which they felt their humanity. He admired the strength in adversity of people like his grandmother: but he abhorred the readiness with which, convinced that they could expect nothing more from life, such people perversely found in suffering the pleasure which under a better social system they would have dis-covered in the normal pastimes and recreations which human beings are equipped by nature to enjoy. Gorky never accused Dostoevsky of lacking compassion for the piteous creatures who abound in his work (indeed, he thought Dostoevsky a more sincerely compassionate man than Tolstoy), but he abhorred the odour of sanctity with which he surrounded these wretches, and he was convinced that the depiction by a writer of genius of the joy which human beings are capable of finding in suffering would encourage many Russian readers to indulge an inborn ten-dency towards self-pity. Such indulgence, in his view, was a particularly repellent manifestation of the passive, ego-centric attitude to life encouraged also by Tolstoyan theories of self-perfection.

Gorky likened 'Karamazovism' to 'Karataevism' because the Dostoevskian cult of suffering in his opinion discouraged active opposition to Tsarism among the Russian reading public as much as Tolstoyan non-resistance to evil. Both encouraged the survival of petty *bourgeois* mentality. In Dostoevsky's work Gorky pointed to Prince Myshkin in *The Idiot* as the character most imbued with the meek unrebellious spirit of Tolstoy's fatalistic peasant. We have seen, however, that he regarded the delight which many Russians seemed to take in inflicting suffering as equally a part of 'Karamazovism' with the pleasure they found in enduring it. Among Dostoevskian characters he found the most complete manifestation of this aspect of Russian psychological illness in old Fyodor Karamazov, who, he said, possessed the evil soul typical of the sort of landowners who amused themselves by hunting their serfs with dogs. He called this kind of behaviour active anarchy, as opposed to the passive anarchy of Karataev. By this he meant that although the streak of sadistic cruelty in the nature of Fyodor Karamazov and others like him was an outgoing force, it sprang nevertheless from the same lack of inner discipline as masochistic self-pity and found expression in actions as senseless and as harmful as those of downtrodden people who deliberately sought opportunities to humiliate themselves. Gorky's broad experience of all spheres of Russian life revealed to him indeed, as to Dostoevsky, that sadism and masochism were often found together in the same person. A particularly striking example of this in his autobiographical novels is his description in *My Apprenticeship* of the behaviour of the passengers on the Volga steamer *Dobry* on which he worked as a galley-boy in the summer of 1881; these people hound and bait a piteous little noncombatant soldier from Vyatka until he is ready to cut his throat from despair, then when the time comes for them to leave the ship they allow themselves to be chased here and there by the crew like a herd of frightened sheep.

Why did these people [writes Gorky] who were capable of tor-
turing a person to the point of madness meekly obey the peremptory
orders of the boat-hands and accept the coarsest vituperation without taking the slightest offence?
Get away from the rails! shouted the boatswain narrowing his
wicked handsome eyes. Can't you see the boat's listing? Beat it, you
devils!
The devils obediently rushed to the other side of the deck. . . .

In his address to the first Congress of Soviet Writers
on 19 August 1934, Gorky attacked the hero of Dostoevsky's
famous *Notes from the Underground* as a 'social degenerate'
in whom his creator showed the 'depths of whining despair
reached by individualists among the ranks of young men of
the nineteenth and twentieth centuries divorced from life'.
Dostoevsky had written that his Underground Man not
only 'could but must inevitably exist in our society in view
of the special circumstances surrounding its formation'; by
this he meant that his hero's rebellion against growing
nineteenth-century prosperity (symbolized by London's
Crystal Palace) was the spontaneous expression of the
eternal longing of the human spirit for freedom from every
kind of servitude—in the mid-nineteenth century from the
servitude of delight in material possessions. In his address
Gorky also declared that the type of the Underground Man
was the product of developing nineteenth-century capitalism, but it was not in his opinion fear of the thraldom of
excessive wealth which provoked the rebellious moods noted
by Dostoevsky, but rather the frustration and disappointment experienced by those who were defeated in the
struggle to acquire wealth—their resentment at failure
found expression, according to their changing moods,
either in bouts of virulent self-pity or in the perpetration
of spiteful actions directed at others.
The difference between Gorky's and Dostoevsky's atti-
tudes to the Underground Man lies not only in their
disagreement as to whether his moods were manifestations

of the eternal human desire for total liberty or merely the product of certain temporary social factors, but also in their divergent concepts of the relationship between will-power and reason. We have seen that one of the tragedies of Russian life, in Gorky's view, was the fact that no social class seemed to him to combine resolution in the pursuit of constructive aims with the power of the disciplined mind which would make the realization of such aims more probable. The intelligentsia lacked the former, the merchantry the latter. The regeneration of Russia required both. Dostoevsky's hero wills himself to commit acts both of sadistic cruelty and of masochistic self-humiliation, and he regards both as equally valuable in themselves, regardless of whether they are intrinsically good or evil, constructive or destructive, precisely because they flow from the assertion of his will-power. The play of his reason, however, inhibits the free exercise of his will-power because it brings to his mind arguments for or against the actions he wishes to perform. Reason stands in the way of his attainment of total liberty of action and he desires therefore to rid himself of it. This divorce of reason from will, in Gorky's view, was precisely the national weakness which prevented the Russian people from realizing their great potential. Gorky objected as much to Dostoevsky's rejection of reason in favour of total liberty of action as he did to Tolstoy's exaltation of natural peasant wisdom over the working of intellect. Yet there lived in him the gloriously irrational figure of the Russian 'ozornik', capable of finding great spiritual solace in acts of sheer destruction.

In the conditions of Tsarist Russian society Gorky's hostility to what seemed to him the socially harmful influence of some of the ideas of Tolstoy and Dostoevsky was not without justification. On the other hand, as we have seen, Dostoevsky fervently proclaimed his hatred of the enslaving effect of *bourgeois* prosperity and *bourgeois* conditional morality upon the human soul; and the patriarchal

Tolstoy despised every manifestation of middle-class life. Gorky was right in attacking the unequal distribution of wealth in the conditions of nineteenth-century capitalism, but mid-twentieth-century experience shows clearly that Dostoevsky was also right in fearing the corruptive effects of widespread affluence. Gorky himself became keenly aware of some of these effects as they showed themselves in Western Europe in the nineteen-twenties, and he would no doubt have discerned their appearance in Soviet society of the nineteen-sixties.

6

In the second part of his autobiographical trilogy, *My Apprenticeship*, Gorky tells us that his first acquaintance with serious literature was made in the spring of 1881 through Mikhail Akimovich Smury, the cook on the Volga steamer, *Dobry*, on which he worked as a galley-boy from May to October of that year. During the next eleven years, before he himself became a writer, Gorky read voraciously everything which came his way, and he gradually formed conclusions about the role of literature in life and about the author's place in society. From the very beginning he found that he instinctively compared life and people in books with life and people as he knew them in reality. He soon became aware of the good writer's power to transform the often repellent material of reality into a captivating fictional picture without sacrificing truth. Reading *Eugénie Grandet*, for example, he spontaneously compared the miser, old Grandet, with his grandfather, but Balzac's artistic creation gave him aesthetic pleasure, whereas Kashirin, in real life inspired him with fear and suspicion. Nevertheless, the very truth of Balzac's portrayal of his miser which gave Gorky great delight, also laid bare the essential evil of Grandet's personality. From such books Gorky became aware of the moral significance of great art as well as of its fascination.

Good books, Gorky perceived, not only presented a gifted artist's captivating view of human life and human beings but also contained their own profoundly true morality; cheap writing, on the other hand, which in his early years came more easily into his possession than good literature, lent support to false standards of behaviour and spurious ethical values. Thus sensational romances always showed the wicked characters as stronger and cleverer than the good, but, for reasons the writers never explained, the latter always won in the end. Gorky knew from bitter experience that in real life good people held their own against the forces of evil only through strenuous effort and that often, despite every effort, they were overcome. Books, therefore, which depicted the mechanical victory of virtue over vice preached a facile, smug morality which repelled him as much as the smug censoriousness of his petty *bourgeois* relations. 'All the authors I had read, except Goncourt, passed judgement on people in the stern, vociferous manner of my employers, often making the reader sympathize with the villains and become exasperated with the good characters.' From a very early age Gorky understood that the unmasking of real wickedness in human behaviour was a task of supreme difficulty even for the great artist, demanding the greatest possible degree of vigilance on his part lest, despite his keen insight and his intuitive wisdom, he should lapse into falsity or hypocrisy.

During the eighteen-nineties, as he gained experience in his new calling as a writer, Gorky gave further intensive thought to the problems of the purpose of literature and of the role of the writer in society—these problems, indeed, preoccupied all Russian writers during that decade. The sum of Gorky's conclusions appeared in an article entitled 'The Reader' which he wrote in 1895 but did not publish until November 1898 in the magazine *Cosmopolis*.

'The Reader' consists of a conversation between a writer returning home from a literary *soirée* and one of his readers who meets him on the way. In a letter to the painter Repin written on 23 November 1899, Gorky explains that the Reader in his sketch is himself, the human being, demanding an account of his work from his other self, the literary artist. The Reader insists that literature must be judged according to the influence it exerts upon the outlook of those for whom it is written. 'The purpose of literature', he declares, 'is to help people to understand themselves, to inspire them with a yearning for truth and to give them greater confidence in themselves; the purpose of literature is to combat human baseness, to reach the good in people and to waken in their souls anger and courage, so that they may become noble and strong and be fired with the sacred principle of beauty.' The Reader reproaches the Writer for falling short of this purpose: 'You are unable to depict life in such a way that your picture will arouse in men a feeling of vengeful shame, a burning desire to create new forms of life.' We see that for Gorky the purpose of literature was both instructive and revolutionary—the writer must not only bring home to his readers the degree to which they have allowed their personality to become corrupted by their surroundings, he must also fire them with a passionate determination to change those surroundings before they are destroyed by them.

Gorky's great contemporary, Chekhov, depicted the imperfections of Russian social life at the end of the nineteenth century with consummate artistry, but his subtle manner of portrayal, based upon suggestive understatement, was ill-suited to inspire his readers with a fervent desire to extirpate the evils he attacked. Gorky loved Chekhov as a man, greatly admired him as an artist, and shared his virulent hatred of the petty *bourgeois* mentality; he was afraid, however, that the very persuasiveness of Chekhov's picture of the moral weaknesses of his generation would so entrance his readers

that they would not draw the correct conclusion from it—
that it was their duty to eradicate their shortcomings and
not simply to contemplate them with pleasure in the work
of a great artist. In a letter to Chekhov, written at the beginning of January 1900, Gorky told his fellow artist: 'It is
absolutely essential that contemporary literature should
begin to embellish life, and as soon as it does so life will
embellish itself, that is people will begin to live at a greater
pace, more brilliantly.' Here Gorky is saying that the creative artist should not allow surrounding reality to dictate the
moral tone of his work; but that he should make a vigorous
assertion of eternal ethical values at the same time that he
reveals how far the life he describes falls short of these
values. The good qualities which in Gorky's opinion many
contemporary people most strikingly lacked were faith in
some great cause and the spiritual valour to dedicate themselves to its fulfilment, albeit at some danger to their
material interests and even, possibly, to their physical
security. In such circumstances it was a writer's duty to
bring before his readers characters who possessed these
virtues, as well as those who were marked by the vices of
the time, and, by setting one against the other, inspire the
readers with such a painful awareness of their personal
moral imperfections that they would no longer be able to
tolerate themselves as they were. Thereafter, when people
had changed, life inevitably would also change.

One might ask at this point whether Gorky's picture of
the filth, brutality, and vileness of lower-class Russian life
was more likely to inspire his readers to reform themselves
than Chekhov's portrayal of middle-class philistinism. To
the evil they depict each writer opposes good qualities—
Chekhov the skill, enlightenment, and devotion of professional men, Gorky scattered gleams of courage, selflessness,
and idealism which might appear in any social class; whereas, however, we feel that the defeat of evil by good in
Chekhov's world will be a slow, uphill process, in Gorky's

work the aggressive intensity of the author's desire that
good should triumph seems to promise that its total victory
will not be long delayed. It may be that the personal circumstances of each writer intrude here—both suffered from
tuberculosis, but whereas Chekhov feared that he was
doomed to an early death, Gorky's magnificent constitution
successfully resisted the disease. Chekhov could not hope to
see a better world in his time; Gorky was determined that
he would.

In 1893, one year after Gorky's debut as a writer, the
critic Dmitri Merezhkovsky, in his long essay 'Reasons for
the decline of contemporary literature and new literary
trends', produced the manifesto of the Russian Modernist
movement. In this essay Merezhkovsky proclaimed beauty
to be the supreme artistic virtue and declared that the
writer's principal purpose should be, not the service of
social good, but the revelation of his own personality. His
work should be judged according to the dual criteria of the
originality and significance of his personal view of life, and
the artistic excellence of his expression of this view. Based
upon individualism and aestheticism, creative literature
would revive in Russia.

Maxim Gorky was hostile to the Russian Modernists.
He regarded their preoccupation with problems of artistic
form as a typical manifestation of the petty *bourgeois* mentality, comparable with the Tolstoyans' trifling with theories
of self-perfection—amusing pastimes which contributed
nothing to the welfare of the Russian people. Gorky's
bitter experience of life had taught him to respect as serious
ideas only those which might help a man to find himself
and to discover his true path in the world. In the early
eighteen-nineties, sitting quietly in a corner, in the salons
of the rich merchants of Nizhny Novgorod, listening to
their teenage children discussing the new poetry, he was
repeatedly tempted to interrupt them with descriptions of
the suffering, both spiritual and physical, which he had

experienced before becoming a writer. Words and ideas, he saw clearly, were only playthings for these comfortably situated young people, and literature no more than a diversion for their leisure time. Gorky in youth had found in books his only source of consolation and encouragement when he was near to despair, and in consequence, when he himself became an author, he tried to write in a manner comprehensible to the simplest of people. He thought that all gifted writers should do this.

The Modernists' interest in the personality of the creative artist was just as repellent to Gorky as their absorption in aesthetic problems. This was not because he was hostile to the principle of individualism as such. He approved, for example, of the self-assertion of business men even though he regarded as immoral their egotistical exploitation of their wealth and power; they were, he recognised, active, dynamic people, and they achieved their success through struggle. In Gorky's view, one of the principal objects of life was struggle, and he thought that a man's character was formed through the resistance he offered to his surroundings. The Modernist poets, however, feared petty *bourgeois* reality because of the possibility that contact with it might harm their poetic sensitivity; and, refusing to struggle with its evils, fled in their work from the depiction of the problems of real life into realms of exotic legend and religious ecstasy. Gorky abhorred such self-indulgence because it seemed to him a further reason to justify a passive attitude to life among intelligent, gifted people who, in his view, should have placed their talents at the service of their humble, suffering compatriots.

During the thirteen years which elapsed between the publication of his first story and the revolution of 1905, Gorky's literary place is among a small group of short-story writers whose work represents the revival of Russian realistic prose fiction after the lull of the eighteen-eighties. The best known of these writers were Alexander Kuprin and Ivan

Bunin, whose first stories appeared respectively in 1889 and 1892. With his emotionally charged view of life, his descriptive force, and the novelty of the milieu he portrayed, Maxim Gorky brought powerful reinforcement to this new realist trend. The three young writers published their stories steadily as the decade advanced, and in their work a second Russian realist school gradually took shape, which, although in certain respects it was permeated with the spirit of Modernism and even made use of some of that movement's stylistic characteristics, stood fundamentally for traditional values in art. In 1897 the collected stories of Kuprin and Bunin were published and the reading public first became aware of the new trend as a consolidated literary school. In the traditional Russian manner, the young writers began to seek points of concentration for their works in organs of the national literary press, and from 1898 to its suppression on 8 June 1901 they published their stories predominantly in the Marxist magazine *Life*, edited by Gorky's friend, Vladimir Posse. This was a natural alliance, since the Marxists, like Maxim Gorky, despised the well-to-do middle-class readers who were the most enthusiastic supporters of the Modernist school. In 1898 the literary battle between Modernists and traditional realists, which was one of the many manifestations of the surging intellectual life of Russian society prior to the revolution of 1905, was decisively joined. The magazine *The World of Art* was founded to champion the Modernist movement, and in 1899 the publishing house 'Scorpion' was set up to publish the works of its adherents. In each year, 1901, 1902, and 1903, this house issued an almanack entitled *Northern Flowers* bringing together for the first time the names of the outstanding young poets. In 1904 'Scorpion' began its own review, *The Scales*, and in it the critic Amfiteatrov called his fellow-Modernists to do battle with the 'barbarians' of the realist school. On their side, the realists were equally active. On 15 May 1898 K. P. Pyatnitsky, G. A. Falburg,

V. I. Charnolussky, V. D. Protopopov, and other ex-members of the Literacy Commission which had been closed down in 1895, requested and obtained permission from the authorities to found the publishing house 'Knowledge', a co-operative in which it was planned that all participating authors should hold shares and take the profit on their own publications. This enterprise was based in St. Petersburg, and at the end of September 1899, on the occasion of his first visit to that city, Gorky became acquainted with Pyatnitsky and joined it as a shareholder. Thereafter it published predominantly the works of the young realists.

The 'Knowledge' enterprise reached the apogee of its influence among the Russian reading public in the years immediately preceding the revolution of 1905; in April 1904 it issued the first of its famous green-backed *Miscellanies*. Forty in all of these *Miscellanies* came out before the organization collapsed through internal dissensions in 1913. Meanwhile, in 1899 in Moscow, the writer N. D. Teleshov (at whose house, in the eighteen-eighties, the literary circle 'Parnassus' had met) with the aid of surviving members of that circle founded the 'Wednesdays' club. The gatherings of this club were attended predominantly by writers of the realist school, and although there were no direct links between it and the 'Knowledge' group, the latter's first *Miscellany* was made up almost entirely of material which had already been read at such gatherings, including Gorky's 'Man'. It was at a 'Wednesdays' meeting on 6 September 1902 that Gorky first read his play *The Lower Depths* to fellow-writers and to artists from the Moscow Arts Theatre.

7

Like most creative artists, Gorky did not easily give sustained allegiance to political parties. In a letter to Chekhov written during the first half of January 1899 he declared: 'I think that all parties are lifeless affairs which contain a good deal more of the self-pride of untalented people than of the spirit of men fired with the desire to build a new, free life for people, upon the ruins of the old, restricted life.' Throughout his life he remained faithful to the conviction expressed here, that political activity exists for the good of the people governed and not for the greater glory of those who govern.

The two principal Russian revolutionary trends during the eighteen-nineties—critical Populism and Marxism—for different reasons both attracted and repelled Gorky. Populist insistence upon the power of the individual to influence the course of history appealed to his admiration for strong, dynamic men, and the readiness of certain members of the Socialist Revolutionary Party to risk their lives in attempts to assassinate prominent personages seemed to him welcome proof that the heroic spirit still existed in contemporary society. On the other hand, his adverse opinion of the Russian peasantry did not predispose him in favour of a party which relied upon them as the instrument of revolution; and the lack among the Populists of a systematically devised plan for revolutionary activity made him suspect that they suffered from the fatal weakness of the traditional Russian intelligentsia—love of theorizing and incapacity for practical planning. The Marxists displeased him because of the less important part—by comparison with the Populists—which they assigned to the individual in the bringing about of revolution, but they attracted him through their demand for a total revolution in Russian life and their possession of a definite tactical plan to achieve it. He particularly liked their intention of making the educated industrial proletariat the instrument of their revolution, because, in his view, such an intention presupposed the transformation of the traditionally drunken, brutish Russian working man into a self-respecting, literate human being.

Gorky's instinctive sympathy for the Marxist cause was intensified during the second half of the eighteen-nineties by the fact that his most devoted friend in literary circles at that time was Vladimir Posse, a prominent Marxist. His earliest direct association with the Marxists dates from the end of September 1899 when during his first visit to St. Petersburg he became the literary editor of their magazine *Life*, of which Posse was the general editor. From this time on he seems to have become more and more favourably disposed to their cause, feeling probably that in view of the growing hostility to Tsarism throughout Russian society he should ally himself with one of the revolutionary parties. His name and literary fame became particularly closely associated with the Marxist movement in April 1901, when their agitators adopted lines from his newly published 'Song of the Stormy Petrel' as rallying cries to inspire revolutionary feeling among the workers. There is some evidence to show that in the years immediately prior to the revolution of 1905 he made financial contributions to Marxist groups in different parts of Russia.

8

Gorky's first meeting with Lenin occurred on 27 November 1905 in the offices of the Marxist magazine *New Life*, prior to a meeting of the Central Committee of the Russian Social Democratic Workers' Party which took place in Gorky's flat at 20 Boulevard Znamenskaya, St. Petersburg. During the next nineteen years, until Lenin's death on 21 January 1924, their relations were marked by the uneasiness one would expect of a relationship between an inflexible, authoritarian politician and an idealistic artist whose most fervent article of faith was a mystical belief in the collective goodness of humanity. The incident which brought out most clearly the gulf between the natures and outlooks of the two men was their dispute over the school for worker propagandists which Gorky directed on Capri from July to December 1909.

One of the results of the failure of the revolution of 1905 was the revival among many Russian intellectuals of that intense preoccupation with religious problems which in Tsarist times persistently asserted itself among thinking people when severe Governmental repressive measures made political activity difficult and dangerous. After 1905 religious enthusiasm reached even the Social Democrats in foreign exile, and provoked among them Lenin's notorious quarrel with the heretical 'God-builders', Bogdanov, Luna-charsky, and others. The fundamental position of the God-builders was that the idea of God was necessary to mankind, but that God, as presented by all established religions, had failed them, and that it was therefore time to create a new God; this new God would not bear the character of a divine being who created men in His image, but would instead be created by men out of the noblest qualities of which through-out the ages humanity had shown itself capable. The resultant composite figure would provide a model of perfec-tion to which all individual men must aspire in their be-haviour on earth, as in the past they had aspired to be united with the perfection of the supernatural God in heaven.

Gorky, living on Capri, responded immediately to the God-builders' ideas. As we have seen, he needed an idea of God to live by, and his childish faith in the God of the Christian Church had been severely shaken by his bitter experience of life and people in his homeland—how could it be, he asked himself, that God created men in his own image when so many specimens of Russian humanity, mutilated physically and spiritually by their harsh condi-tions of life, were but caricatures of men? It pleased him to think of God as a model of perfection to which men might attain on earth because such an idea served the only cause which he considered truly sacred and great—the cause of the never-ending physical, spiritual, and intellectual de-velopment of Man. The object of his Capri school was to acquaint his worker pupils with the loftiest manifestations of human endeavour throughout the ages and by thus building the figure of his God before their eyes inspire them with the desire to achieve the perfection embodied in this figure. They would then march in the vanguard of the revolution. Later, by means of education, the masses would be raised to their level.

The purpose of Gorky's Capri school was to unite a religious ideal with a revolutionary design. It is typical of his political *naïveté* that he could have entertained even the faintest hope of enlisting Lenin's support for such an enterprise. Lenin was an authoritarian who despised the collective humanity which Gorky idealized and a complete materialist who evaluated all religious thinking from the point of view of its social and political implications. He regarded the idea of God as the incarnation of the highest potentialities of human nature as no less pernicious than the traditional concept of a supernatural deity. Gorky's school opened on 24 July 1909 with the arrival of fifteen selected workers from Russia, and from the start Lenin attacked it mercilessly as harmful fractional activity and urged the pupils to abandon it and to visit him in Paris before returning to Russia. On 10 November five of them left Capri and on the 13th they were followed to Paris by their leader, Vilonov. On 20 December the remaining students completed their course and also left the island for Paris. Having rendered Gorky's school ineffective Lenin visited the writer on Capri on 1 July 1910 and friendly relations between the two men were re-established. Lenin valued Gorky, the writer of *Mother*, too highly as a collaborator in the cause of proletarian revolution to allow protracted hostility to exist between them.

Gorky's religious aspirations were fundamental to his nature and stayed with him to the end of his life. It is striking that Ilya Lunyev, the hero of his novel *The Three of Them*, sees the falsity of his commercial ambitions most clearly when he is sitting in church. Four years after the incident of the Capri school Gorky's persistent religious idealism again provoked Lenin's furious anger. In the open letter 'More on Karamazovism' which he sent on 27 October 1913 to the newspaper *The Russian Word* Gorky let fall the sentence: 'As for the quest for God, it must be put aside for a while.' In a letter of 14 November Lenin violently attacked his friend's implication that the idea of God must be abandoned in Russian life only 'for a while' and fulminated against his incorrigible leaning towards religious concepts: 'A Catholic priest' he wrote 'who violates young girls is considerably less dangerous to democracy than a priest without a surplice, a priest without a crude religion, a democratic priest of ideas who preaches the building and creating of a petty God.' This letter was followed by a second a few days later, equally abusive, in which Lenin accused Gorky of supporting the cause of reaction through his preoccupation with the idea of God. This accusation aroused the idealistic writer's indignation, and relations between the two men were disrupted for five years.

Gorky's plan to produce a revolutionary working class *élite* through the application of God-building theories was closely linked with his abiding conviction that successful revolution could only be brought about through an alliance between educated workers and the traditional intellectual forces of his country. He saw God-building as essentially an instrument for the transformation of men through education. The man therefore who in 1917–18 in his newspaper *New Life* called insistently for the cultural elevation of the people, and thereby once again involved Lenin's displeasure, was the same who had clashed with the Bolshevik leader over the educational aims of the Capri school.

9

Gorky was an example of a not infrequent phenomenon— a creative artist whose ideas sprang from his emotions rather than his reason. His attachment to 'God-building' theories was the nearest he came to adopting a coherent system of philosophy. This attachment sprang from his hatred of the manner in which the bestial conditions of lower class Russian life mutilated his fellow creatures both physically and spiritually and frustrated the development of their best human potentialities. Faced in real life with innumerable specimens of human degradation he cherished the idea of God as the embodiment of the loftiest possibilities of human nature. Gorky's most characteristic ideas are contained in his criticisms of the moral influence of Tolstoy and Dostoevsky upon the Russian intelligentsia, and these were inspired by his temperamental antipathy to passive, self-pitying people. Gorky's best works are based not upon ideas but upon intuition and observation; Pritchett aptly describes him as 'a powerful, blind man being led by a voracious, allseeing child'.

2. THE SHORT STORY

I

DURING his youthful wanderings Maxim Gorky was an indefatigable collector of folk legends. When he became a writer, convinced of the didactic purpose of literature, he had recourse to his knowledge of folk-lore to assist him in communicating to his readers the moral lessons he wished to teach them. He did not, however, think that the legends were in themselves sources of perfect wisdom. He once told his friend Vasili Desnitsky that he thought it pointless simply to write down what he had heard, in the form in which he had heard it. By this he meant that he so adapted the legends he retold that the message he wished to communicate to his readers flowed naturally from them. Unfortunately none of the legends he wrote up in this way have reached us in their original form, and we cannot, therefore, study the changes his didactic purpose led him to make.

The two early stories in which Gorky made the most striking use of folk legend are 'Makar Chudra' (1892) and 'Old Izergil' (1894). In these stories Gorky, the narrator, presents himself as a wanderer who stops and sits for a while, somewhere in the southern steppe, near the sea, with Makar Chudra, an old gypsy, and Izergil, a Bessarabian hag; he makes these two exotic characters relate to him the inspiring legends with which he wishes to acquaint his readers. Chudra tells the tale of the great love of the beautiful Radda and the proud Loiko Zobar which ends in the death of both, presenting it not as a legend but as an adventure which happened among his own tribe, to which

Radda once belonged. Izergil tells of Larra, half-eagle, half-man, condemned to eternal wandering because he murders a girl in his mother's tribe who spurns his love; and of Danko, the great leader, who, out of love for mankind, leads his tribe through a dark forest by the light of his burning heart, and falls dead when they safely reach the other side. These events occurred long, long ago, but Izergil attaches them to the present by telling her listener that a dark shape he sees in the steppe is Larra's wandering shadow, and that blue will-o'-the-wisps are sparks from Danko's heart. For Gorky legends were only valuable in so far as the lessons to be learned from them could be applied to contemporary reality.

Gorky opens the story of his brief encounter with Makar Chudra with a conversation between Chudra and himself as the narrator. This conversation did not take place in reality as he describes it in the story, for it is in fact a dialogue between two sides of his own nature. Its theme is one which preoccupied him throughout his formative years —should a strong, resilient young man like himself, capable of withstanding every hardship life offered, concern himself about weaker beings and try to help them, or should he devote all his strength to his own advancement and to the enjoyment of the numerous pleasures the world contains? The narrator, a wandering intellectual, favours the first alternative, but Chudra, a wild, freedom-loving gypsy, declares himself forcibly for the second. In his view, strong men who worry about other people and seek a moral purpose in life succeed only in destroying their delight in it, for life is meant to be lived with all the vitality a man possesses, and not thought about. It is fruitless for clever people to try to teach others how to live, for there is nothing to teach. 'Everyone knows what his needs are' affirms Chudra; 'the bright ones grab all that's going, the rest get nothing, and so everyone teaches himself.' Despite the amoral egotism of his gypsy's outlook, Gorky, in 1892 was taken with it, and he recommends it to his readers' sympathy. It pleased him because at that time he prided himself upon the physical and spiritual strength with which he had met and overcome the tribulations of his early life. Like Chudra, old Izergil not only relates to her young listener her favourite legends, but also expresses to him her views on life and people; and, like Chudra's, her views are Gorky's at the time he wrote the story. 'Old Izergil' was written almost three years after 'Makar Chudra', and during those years Gorky had developed from a vagrant odd-job man into a person convinced that his life's vocation was to be a writer; this new sense of purpose reveals itself in the fact that Chudra's crude hedonism is replaced in Izergil with the belief that a man must live his life in such a way that, when he dies, he will leave behind him some mark of his existence. With this more rational view of the purpose of life Izergil combines a less anarchical attitude than Chudra's to the quality they both most admire in human beings—strength; for Chudra strength means the service of self and the absolute rejection of all obligations to society and people, but Izergil recognizes strong men—of whom, she says, there are few in contemporary society—by their determination to impose their will upon the course of events, and not, like the great majority of human beings, passively reconcile themselves to whatever, by chance, happens around them. Izergil's viewpoint stands between that of Chudra and the narrator's; like Chudra, she regards strong men as laws unto themselves, but the fact that she sees the purpose of life in achievement shows that she expects them to work and therefore to contribute to human welfare.

Gorky's changing attitude, during the first half of the eighteen-nineties, to the relationship between strong men and the rest of humanity is revealed not only in the different opinions of Chudra and Izergil on this subject, but also in the clash between Chudra's views and the lessons contained in Izergil's legends of Larra and Danko. Larra, the son of an eagle (which, though noble, is nevertheless a bird of prey) and a woman, falls in love with a girl of his mother's tribe and, when she rejects his love, murders her; in the mood in which he wrote his earlier story, Gorky would have approved such a deed because it is inspired by powerful emotion, but in Izergil's tale, Larra is punished not only by being driven from his tribe but also through being deprived of the ability to die, so that his lonely wandering will be eternal. In her second legend, in contrast with Larra, the rapacious individualist, Izergil tells of the martyr Danko, who gives his life for his people and by so doing shows that, contrary to Chudra's assertion, the strong man's duty is to concern himself with the fate of his weaker fellow-creatures, regardless of their cowardice and lack of gratitude. From the events of these legends we see that, whereas in his vagrant days Gorky regarded strength as good in itself, to whatever ends it might be applied, by 1894 he has modified this view; he now condemns the strong man who exploits and preys upon humanity, but sees as truly great the leader who places his qualities of mind and character at their service.

As a literary character Makar Chudra suffers from the marked weakness that behind his wild, untutored façade the reader is too strongly aware of the personality of Alexei Peshkov, the vagrant intellectual, confused by the contradictions between the teaching of imperfectly understood books and the lessons of experience. This incongruity was the price Gorky paid for wishing to enlist his readers' sympathy for his views through attaching them to picturesque, romantic characters. 'Old Izergil' is incomparably superior to 'Makar Chudra' as a short story because, although not unblemished by Gorky's persistent urge to philosophize, Izergil, to a much greater extent than Chudra, is a living person in her own right, and not merely the mouthpiece for her creator's views. When we meet her she is over seventy and hideously ugly; but in the tales she tells her young listener of her numerous love affairs between the ages of fifteen and forty she appears as a vital, proud, and beautiful young girl like Chudra's Radda. In her twenties and thirties she always thought more highly of herself than of her lovers and sent them packing when she tired of them. At the age of forty, however, she met a Polish gentleman, Arkadek, with whom, for the first time in her life, she fell sincerely in love and wished to settle down. But by then her beauty had faded, and Arkadek rejects her love. Time thus punishes her for her arrogant behaviour in youth.

The story 'Old Izergil' is linked with Gorky's autobiographical sketch 'First Love' (1922). This sketch tells of his love affair with the wife of a Polish revolutionary Olga Yulevna Kaminskaya, five years his senior. He met this woman first in Nizhny Novgorod in June 1889 but at that time she refused to leave her husband to live with him. He re-met her in September 1892 in Tiflis and she and her daughter Olga came to join him in Nizhny Novgorod in December. They lived together until December 1894.

In youth Gorky was a romantic idealist about sexual love. He derived the greatest pleasure in his relationship with Kaminskaya from a feeling that he was protecting her and her little girl from the harshness of life. Kaminskaya, on the other hand, was a sensualist and before meeting Gorky she had had love affairs in several European capitals. From her wandering, knock-about life she had fashioned a crude, uncomplicated outlook—life is simple but sometimes rough, its only problem is to know how to smooth out the rough places. This down-to-earth philosophy much attracted Gorky when he got to know her because he was then in a state of agonizing mental turmoil from thinking too much about the 'cursed questions'—in his case the meaning of life and his place in it. This mental agony had caused him to attempt suicide in 1887. His disillusionment in his mistress started when one day she told him that the best lovers were Frenchmen, and from then on he became more and more scandalized by her cynical descriptions of her earlier affairs.

Gorky wrote 'Old Izergil' in the autumn of 1894, when his relationship with Kaminskaya was coming to an end. He expresses his moral disapproval of all promiscuous young women like her through the contrast he draws between the spirited, much-desired Izergil in youth and her loneliness and repulsive appearance in old age. The reader naturally compares her situation with that of her predatory hero of legend, Larra, condemned through excessive pride to wander the earth alone for ever. A lifelong incorrigible moralist, Gorky conceived Izergil as a warning to his loose-living mistress of what might befall her in old age if she did not mend her ways. She would be left destitute and friendless once she had lost the attractions of youth.

Usually critical of his own work, Gorky congratulated himself in later life upon the harmonious manner in which he combined in the figure of Izergil a lesson in personal morality with social criticism. He achieved this with natural-ness through making his lonely aged heroine (as old folk often do) compare unfavourably the people she now sees around her with those she knew in her halcyon years. 'In those days', she says, 'in my time, people had more strength and fire about them and this made life gayer and better.' In this nostalgic backward glance of an old woman at the time of her youth, thirty to forty years ago (ie. to the eighteen-fifties and sixties) Gorky expresses his personal disapproval of some of the prevailing moods in Russian society of the eighteen-eighties and early eighteen-nineties which he had already condemned in his allegory of the Siskin and the Woodpecker (see page 35). He looks back with regret to patriarchal times when Russian people were less corrupted by commercialism and when the intellectuals were concerned with great humanistic and revolutionary ideas. Regret for the old days may seem strange in a man of

Gorky's outlook but it was a feeling he shared with many radical thinkers and writers of the end of the nineteenth century. The figure of Izergil is a good example of Gorky's ability —to use Belinsky's phrase—'to think in human images'. At times the voice of the pedantic, moralizing young writer behind her is intrusive but in general her strictures on contemporary Russian people flow naturally from the philosophy of life which she expounds as she tells her listener stories of her early years. She is a successful artistic creation whose convincingness as a personality is not destroyed by Gorky's didactic purpose. The harmonious blending of didacticism with art is a difficult task and Gorky deserves praise for the skill with which in Old Izergil, at so early a stage in his career, he performs it.

2

Despite the admixture of reality provided by Izergil's story of her youthful love affairs, the tale as a whole remains outside everyday Russian life. Through his heroine's critical attitude to contemporary people, and the lessons contained in her legends, Gorky could show how far in his view real life fell short of the ideal; but so long as he confined his action to the steppe he could not depict urban life as he knew it. This irked him because his genius was essentially realistic. Yet his temperament was such that he was incapable of writing of a reality which he hated without challenging it. By the middle of the eighteen-nineties, therefore, he began to look for a means of expressing the protest of Chudra and Izergil in a literary character who, instead of merely, like them, uttering criticisms of surrounding life, could be brought naturally into contact with people and demonstrate his disapproval of them through his behaviour. In Gorky's experience the town dweller who could most convincingly be made to speak with the voice of his wandering gypsies was the down-and-out, with whom during his vagrant formative years he had felt he had much in common. Such people lived near enough to the Russian reading public in the towns for the latter to feel that the views they expressed might have some relevance to their own everyday experience; but at the same time they were remote enough from polite society for Gorky to be able to dress up their vagabond psychology as romantic tilting at petty *bourgeois* windmills without offending his reader's sense of the probable. He was intensely interested in them as human beings, and he knew them better than any Russian writer who had yet written about them. In every way, therefore, they were the perfect prototypes for the creation of a literary character who, would be rooted in reality, and yet could be elevated by Gorky's stylistic skill into a romantic protest. The first story in which Gorky portrayed such a character in such a way was 'Chelkash', published in the Populist magazine *Russian Wealth* for June 1895. It was his first work to appear in a literary organ of national repute.

'Chelkash' was written in the summer of 1894, before 'Old Izergil', which was written in the autumn. This shows that even while Gorky was imaginatively occupied with legendary champions of pride and freedom, he was already turning to the problem of finding their prototypes in real life—to the traditional search of the Russian writer for a positive hero.

The abandonment of the impoverished countryside by thousands of ex-serfs in search of a livelihood in the cities, and their slow, painful psychological adjustment to urban life, is one of the dominant facts of Russian social history in the second half of the nineteenth century. The plot of 'Chelkash' is based upon this phenomenon. On the docks of a large Russian port we meet Grisha Chelkash, an ex-peasant who left his native village eleven years before the story opens and earns his living by smuggling and theft.

His usual accomplice, Misha, has a broken leg and he replaces him on a smuggling expedition with Gavrila, a peasant youth fresh from the countryside, whom he meets one day by accident outside the dock gates. Their expedition is successful, but they quarrel about the sharing of the booty. Chelkash keeps only one note and contemptuously throws the rest at Gavrila. They part.

'Chelkash' consists of four parts. The first is a short introductory sketch describing activity on the docks on a typical working day and emphasizing the puniness of men beside the enormous machines they have themselves created. The second introduces the hero, Chelkash, contrasts his swashbuckling, freedom-loving nature with the slaves of industry described in the opening sketch, and relates his encounter with Gavrila and his enlistment of him as his new assistant. The third recounts the smuggling expedition, and the fourth the quarrel about the booty, which takes place on a desolate stretch of sand. Each part is complete in itself, but each one contributes to the organic unity of the story as a whole.

The interest of 'Chelkash' lies principally in the contrast drawn by the author between the behaviour of his two protagonists; this contrast is pointed by the fact that both are of peasant origin, but eleven years of urban life have wrought some degree of change in Chelkash, whereas Gavrila is still fundamentally the peasant he was born. Gorky is here on firm realistic ground. Through an objective comparison of Chelkash and Gavrila he could have shown typical changes which took place in the mentality of the numerous Russian serfs who, after their emancipation in 1861, abandoned the villages inhabited by their ancestors for hundreds of years and arriving in the towns developed into restless urban *déracinés*. It was not, however, Gorky's purpose in his story to make a comparative psychological study of his two heroes, presenting them as types of thousands of their countrymen at a precise historical moment; but rather to depict, in their short relationship, the clash between the eternally free human spirit and the soul of contemporary Russian people, enslaved by the shibboleths of both the old and the new social orders. Chelkash and Gavrila are thus not types but symbols, and it was for this reason that the editorial board of the Populist *Russian Wealth* (instinctively unsympathetic to Gorky's hostile portrayal of Gavrila's peasant mentality) were justified in first rejecting 'Chelkash' on the grounds that the characters were too abstract. After Gorky had made certain changes in the story they were persuaded by his mentor Korolenko to reverse their decision; but the dispute between the two accomplices over the proceeds of their expedition remains a clash between opposed human qualities rather than between two individuals. In Gavrila, the peasant, Gorky embodies what in his view were the worst moral vices widespread in all classes of late nineteenth-century Russian society—excessive caution, worship of money, cowardice, and opportunism; in addition Gavrila retains the superstition and exaggerated respect for religious forms which spring from his peasant origin. Chelkash, the thief, in contrast, reveals the virtues which the writer considered human beings should at all costs preserve, despite the corruptive influence of their surroundings—independence of spirit, courage, love of adventure, and contempt for financial gain. 'Chelkash' is less a story than a parable, but it is an extremely well-told parable.

'Chelkash' opens with the description of an everyday scene in a Russian port, but ends with a fight between the two heroes on a desolate stretch of sand which might be anywhere. Because this fight is a dramatic clash between eternal and universal human qualities, its location is unimportant, and the stretch of sand is, in fact, only a stage upon which Gorky makes his two symbolic characters play out the climax of the dramatic conflict which has been maturing between them from the beginning of the story. At the end of their altercation Chelkash and Gavrila leave the spot as if they were actors leaving a stage, Chelkash in one direction and Gavrila in the other—to opposite wings —and the manner of their departures sums up the impression which throughout the narrative Gorky has been trying to make each produce upon the reader. Chelkash staggers away, like a wounded hero, holding his bleeding head with one hand and smoothing his moustaches with the other; Gavrila crosses himself, places his money inside his shirt, and quickly walks off—the slave to both God and Mammon.

The symbolic characterization which Gorky employs in his depiction of Chelkash is one of the most typical features of his work as a whole. We find it still in his last long work, the novel *Klim Samgin*. Its weakness as a literary method was that, in order to express abstract concepts through his fictional characters, Gorky was often obliged to resort to false psychology, a failing which particularly displeased Tolstoy in his early stories. Chelkash was based upon a hobo whom Gorky met as a patient in the next bed to his in hospital in the town of Nikolaev and who recounted to him the incident around which he constructed his story. As a finished literary figure Chelkash bears a certain general resemblance to people like his real-life original, but the latter, if he had read the story, would have been astonished at the motives of behaviour which Gorky attributed to his hero, and he would not have recognized himself in some of Chelkash's actions. Chelkash, for example, will not work because he refuses to barter his freedom for money, he boasts that by coming to the town he has cast off the age-old bonds of village life, and he commits crimes from love of adventure and as a gesture of defiance to accepted canons of morality. His real-life prototypes did not work, either out of idleness or because employment in the towns was often impossible to obtain; having abandoned their native villages because of poverty many of them found they were no better off in the town, and, far from enjoying greater liberty, they were exploited by employers to a degree their ancestors

had never known under their rustic masters; and they became criminals in despair of finding any other way in which
to keep themselves alive. It is most unlikely that, having
successfully completed a smuggling expedition, a typical
hobo would have thrown almost all the money he had gained
from it at his accomplice and felt himself to be a hero in
doing so. Nor, when the latter, in an attempt to seize all
the money, had felled him with a stone, would he, like
Chelkash, have forgiven him on the grounds that even if the
stone had killed him, he would have been no loss to society.
Later in life Gorky confessed that the hobos he knew personally were much more fearsome people than those he presented
in his stories. Alexei Tolstoy picturesquely described the
latter as 'dream-hobos'.

When Korolenko read 'Chelkash', he exclaimed: 'Wonder-
ful—didn't I tell you you were a realist?'—but, after a
moment's thought, added: 'but, at the same time, a
romantic.' Korolenko had himself written stories about
hobos and he knew them well enough to understand that
in Chelkash Gorky was striving to present an amoral, root-
less vagrant to his readers as an heroic symbol of ideal
human behaviour. He saw also, however, that in doing this
his young protégé was pursuing a conscious didactic purpose, was not deceived about the true nature of his hero,
and, with the Russian writer's traditional respect for truth,
felt obliged to reveal it, even at the risk of prejudicing the
instructional value of his story. Gorky's exaltation of his
ragged champion of strength and freedom reaches its apogee
when, their expedition safely concluded, Chelkash and Gavrila are rowing slowly back to the shore. The perils of the
past night have completely unmanned Gavrila: 'He rowed
mechanically, all huddled up, as if expecting a blow to fall
upon him from above; not a desire, not a single emotion
remained in him, he felt empty and spiritless. The excitement of the night had sucked everything human out of
him.' Chelkash, in contrast, at this moment is confident,

relaxed, and exultant. 'His nerves, accustomed to excitement, were already placid again. His moustaches quivered with delight and his eyes shone. He felt magnificent, whistled through his teeth, drew deep breaths of the moist sea air, looked round him and smiled good-naturedly when his eyes lighted upon Gavrila.' Pleased with his night's work, Chelkash takes pity upon his terrified young companion, and to calm him begins to exchange with him reminiscences of country life. Memories of childhood help to assuage Gavrila's fears, as Chelkash had hoped, but their effect upon Chelkash himself is unexpected; slowly, as he talks, his carefully cherished illusion that he had left behind the complete servitude of rustic life for the absolute freedom of the town yields to an affectionate remembrance of the particular kind of liberty he had known as a peasant youth: 'The chief thing in the life of a peasant [he tells Gavrila] is liberty. You are your own master. You have your house— not worth a farthing, perhaps—but still your own. You have your land—a mere handful, no doubt—but yours none the less. You have your own hives, your own eggs, your own apples. You are king on your own land.' Gavrila watches with surprise as the arrogant, devil-may-care urban rapscallion he had imagined Chelkash to be is overcome before his eyes by nostalgic regret for the countryside of which up to then he had spoken with nothing but contempt. Chelkash, for his part, is so strongly affected by his memories that he loses control of the skiff which earlier he had managed with the effortless mastery appropriate to the splendid hero Gorky had represented him to be. The skiff drifts at the caprice of the waves. 'The waves seemed to understand that the skiff had lost purpose, and pitching it higher and higher, began lightly to sport with it, flashing their friendly blue fire beneath its oars.'

The change in the movement of Chelkash's skiff from firmly directed progress towards the shore to aimless drifting has a symbolic meaning. In his moment of weakness

Chelkash reveals himself in his true character—an uprooted vagrant tossed in every direction by the arbitrary course of historical events, and not a hero of his time, in absolute control of his own destiny and impervious because of the strength of his personality to the baleful influence of his surroundings. At the end of this episode Chelkash and Gavrila fall asleep in the hold of a barque. 'The barque rocked gently upon the heaving water, here and there a plank gave a melancholy squeak, the rain fell softly on the deck and the waves lapped the side of the vessel. It was all very mournful and sounded like the cradle-song of a mother devoid of hope for the happiness of her son.' Let Chelkash make what defiant gestures he pleases—he is not an heroic but a tragic figure, torn from his ancestral past in a patriarchal village and destined, as he grows older, to perish in an urban slum. His successors in Gorky's work inhabit the doss-house of *The Lower Depths*.

3

'Chelkash' is the only story in which, despite his clear perception of the worthlessness of his ragged hero, Gorky nevertheless succeeded in presenting him to his readers as an heroic symbol. In later stories with a vagrant as the central character he abandons his romantic attempt to elevate the vices of restlessness and cynicism into the virtues of love of freedom and contempt for conventional morality, and analyses the nature of his hero's emotional instability, as earlier Russian writers, even though sympathetic to the superfluous man, had attempted to establish the reasons for his spiritual malaise. Two such stories are 'Konovalov' (1896) and 'A Rolling Stone' (1897). The structure of these stories is similar. The author, in the course of his wanderings, meets two vagrants, Alexander Ivanovich Konovalov, a baker from Murom, and Pavel Ignatiev Promtov, of noble birth, and listens to their life-stories and their views on life. Both these men, of widely differing backgrounds, suffer from a common emotional illness—recurring attacks of virulent depression which are the basic reason for their ceaseless wandering. Promtov describes the nature of these attacks. 'Everything around you loses its interest and you desire something new. You cast about here, there and everywhere, you look and look, and finally you find something which you seize upon, only to discover at once that it is not what you wanted. You feel yourself in the power of some dark monster, you feel spiritually bound, incapable of living with yourself . . . a wretched state of affairs.' For Konovalov when he is in this emotional state, the whole of humanity is repugnant: 'let them all die—it won't worry me.' He finds relief in drink and vagrancy. 'On and on you travel—always something new to see. Your mind's a blank. The wind blows in your face and clears all kinds of filth from your soul.' Painfully aware of his illness, Konovalov blames no one for it, and he is sorry for the women who have loved him but with whom his wayward temperament would not allow him to settle down. The intellectual, Gorky, suggests that perhaps he, and others like him, are the victims of the monstrous injustices suffered in the course of Russian history by people of his class, but Konovalov will have none of this: his brother—he says—has the same historical background, yet he manages a successful bakery. He listens with contempt to the complaints of his fellow-lodgers in doss-houses that Fate is responsible for their misfortunes—where were you, he asks, when your fate was decided?

Konovalov is described by Gorky as 'one of those brooding people who abound in Russian life and who are more unhappy than anyone else because the oppressiveness of their thoughts is intensified by the blindness of their mind'. Promtov, on the other hand, is an intellectual. Gorky modelled him upon a Petersburg schoolmaster. Positive and negative elements are fairly well balanced in his outlook, which rests on some semblance of amoral logic; positive are his contempt for book wisdom, disapproval for people who habitually allow their hearts to rule their heads, refusal to complain if he is caught and severely punished for his vagrant felonies; negative are his tendency to depression, a sadistic fondness for making women suffer, a passion for gambling, admiration for downright dishonesty in preference to conditional morality. The decisive weakness of Promtov's personality is that he cannot control his emotional instability, and his boast, therefore, that 'my mind and my emotions are in perfect harmony'—the mark of the superman—cannot be maintained; he marries, for example, in a fit of restless depression, then leaves his wife. Most typically Gorkian in him is his polemic with Tolstoyan theories of self-perfection, which, he considers, undermine the wholeness of the personality—'why drag yourself by the tail to the left when your nature with all her might pushes you to the right?' Promtov believes that a man should not squander his energy in self-interrogation but that he should be what his strongest impulses make him and that he should accept himself as such without self-torment. This for him is the highest level of human nature.

The dethronement of the freedom-loving hero in Chelkash by the restless melancholic in Konovalov is clearly visible if we compare the two. Chelkash will not work because to do so will reduce him to the level of the wretched dockers, slaves of their machines; he first asserts his superiority over Gavrila by showing how much greater is his capacity for alcohol. Konovalov is a highly skilled baker, loves his work, and only leaves it because of his emotional instability; he does not regard heavy drinking as a virtue but drinks to relieve his attacks of depression. When Chelkash throws his bank-notes—the proceeds of the smuggling expedition—at Gavrila, he 'felt himself a hero', and looking at his companion he rejoices that, *déraciné* though he is, he will never allow himself to be so enslaved by financial greed; Konovalov deserts a wealthy business woman who wishes to keep him, but he does so not out of contempt for money, but because he is temperamentally incapable of living permanently with anyone. Holding his wounded head, Chelkash stalks out of his story to where new adventures await his skill and courage; Konovalov hangs himself from the stove vent in gaol at the age of forty. Promtov, the amoral apostle of the harmonious personality, with lurking, fatal weaknesses of temperament, reminds us strongly of Lermontov's Pechorin. Most compellingly one thinks of Lermontov's hero as one reads of the pleasure Promtov finds in swindling peasants out of a few coppers, a pursuit as derisory for the strong man as Pechorin's endless trivial love affairs. Konovalov, on the other hand, belongs to the lineage of Oblomov and Rudin; the fine words are there, the better impulses, but they are all heroes for a single hour and they all perish. Both Promtov and Konovalov are based on real-life prototypes, but in each of them we recognize familiar characteristics of their creator, himself a vagrant spiritually and physically until he at last found his path in life as a writer. From himself to both Gorky gave the strong tendency to depression which once caused him to attempt suicide; to Promtov, in addition, he gave his hatred of Tolstoyan theories of self-perfection, his contempt for grey morality, his desire for personal harmony, to Konovalov his refusal to accept Fate as an instrument of human destiny, his compassion for suffering, his respect for work. Endowing his fictional characters with these qualities which he admired in himself, Gorky yet withheld from them his unique writer's genius, and without that they remain 'superfluous men'. In Konovalov's words, strikingly reminiscent of Oblomov's: 'There are a lot of people like me. We are folk of a special kind, we don't fit in anywhere. A census should be taken of us and laws passed to get rid of us—very strict laws. Because we're no good to anyone yet we take up space and get in other people's way.'

Chelkash, Promtov, and Konovalov are all men who have

cast off the bonds of established life and become confirmed vagrants. In 'The Orlovs' (1897) Gorky relates the last few months in the life of the cobbler Grigori Orlov before he yields to the inborn unrest in his nature and joins the 'barefoot battalion' of the down-and-outs. These months bring about the break-up of his marriage to his wife Matryona, whom he had married three years before the story opens. These years have been a period of steady deterioration in their relationship, which Gorky attributes to the destitution of lower-class urban Russian life. 'They had no experiences or interests which might have given them a chance to rest from each other or satisfied a natural human need for excitement and reflection, a need, in a word, for life.' Gorky begins his narrative at the point when their parting seems imminent although their love is not yet dead: '. . . these fundamentally decent people lived from day to day waiting for something which would finally smash to smithereens their agonizing, senseless life.' This decisive incident occurs, but its immediate effect is not to destroy but temporarily to cement their union. The great cholera epidemic of 1891 reaches their town and they both volunteer to work as orderlies in the local hospital. This useful activity provides the sense of purpose which their lives had previously lacked, they become happier, and their relationship improves. After a short while, however, Orlov's temperamental unrest asserts itself; he becomes disillusioned with the menial tasks the hospital imposes upon him when he feels he is capable of so much greater things, throws up the work in disgust, and departs for the doss-house which he never again leaves. After the epidemic, the hospital superintendent finds Matryona employment as a teacher of shoe-making in a technical institute, but she is seriously ill with consumption caused by earlier malnutrition and she is doomed to an early death. Thus the story ends with the moral destruction of one of these fine young people and the imminent physical destruction of the other. This is the only one of his early stories in which Gorky

shows one of his neurotic heroes in a close personal relationship with a person of stable temperament. Matryona Orlova
is a tragic figure who perishes because she married Orlov.
She is superior to the average woman of her class and could
have become a useful member of society. Orlov is not tragic
but tragi-comic. The key to Gorky's attitude to his hero
appears in the manner in which the hospital superintendent
takes his leave of him as he strides defiantly out of the
building: 'Good-bye, tragedian,' he shouts. To this ration-
ally minded doctor, his rebellious orderly seems to be play-
acting. The doctor does not appreciate the fact that he is
dealing with a man of such unbalanced temperament that
the mere suspicion that he can be at all useful inspires him
with delusions of grandeur. Finding that he can help
cholera victims in small ways, Orlov conceives the ambition of ridding Russia of the disease for ever. There are elements of tragedy in him because his unstable nature makes
his doom inescapable, but his attempts to rationalize his
behaviour are laughable. Sometimes he speaks with his
creator's voice (when, for example, he declares that he has
no intention of folding his arms and waiting to be overtaken
by cholera), but in joining the army of down-and-outs he
takes the step which, Gorky tells us, in moods of despair, he
himself was tempted to take, but did not, because he was
convinced that a man must resist the influence of his surroundings, not yield to it. No one will profit from Orlov's
venomous imprecations from his corner in the doss-house.
Gorky knew that the true path for the man disgusted with
life around him ('surely something better than this could
be arranged!' Orlov exclaims) was that of the active refor-
mer or revolutionary, not the nihilistic withdrawal of the
disgruntled intellectual unable to find the opportunity he
desires to perform gigantic tasks in the world.

Throughout these early stories it is evident that Gorky's
ragged heroes are spoiling for a fight with established society.
This fight finally occurs in 'Creatures that Once were Men'

(1897). In this story Aristide Kuvalda, an ex-army officer who is now the drunken owner of a doss-house, pits his wits against the businessmen, Petunnikov father and son, in a lawsuit. The degeneration of the heroic protest of Chudra and Izergil against *bourgeois* ethics emerges clearly in the fact that after only six years their successor in Gorky's work, Kuvalda, throws down his challenge to the masters of commercial society in the form of a legal quibble. Petunnikov senior, an old-style merchant, is nonplussed by his enemy's action, but his son, a Europeanized businessman in the late nineteenth-century style, in checked suit instead of caftan, has no difficulty in defeating his enemy through bribery and cunning. 'The clever ones,' said Chudra, 'grab what's going, the rest get nothing.' Settlement is made for a few roubles with which Kuvalda buys vodka and some scraps of food for himself and his lodgers; they consume them in the courtyard, and the spectacle they present at their paupers' feast sums up Gorky's dethronement of his swashbuckling Nietzschean vagrant in the same way as the spectacle of Oblomov lying on Pshenitsyna's sofa summed up Goncharov's dethronement of the Byronic 'superfluous man': 'they sat and lay in various postures and their rags made them look like ugly animals, created by a crude, fantastic force as a joke on mankind.'

4

A considerable number of Gorky's early stories are written in the first person although in some of these (e.g. 'The Affair with the Clasps') the narrator's part in events is insignificant. Two stories in which the teller's rôle is essential to the working out of the basic theme are 'At the Salt Marsh' (1895) and 'My Fellow-Traveller' (1894). In each of these tales Gorky presents himself with roughly the same identity—that of an earnest young wandering intellectual who encounters people who have never heard of theories of morality, and whose views of right and wrong are wholly conditioned by their life experience. The dramatic impact of the story springs from the resultant clash of personalities.

'At the Salt Marsh' is based upon an incident which occurred in July–August 1891 at Ochakov, near Odessa, where Gorky worked for a short while with salt-miners. The narrator wears spectacles, a fact which betrays him to the miners as an intellectual. As he approaches, his appearance arouses their spontaneous hostility and one of them, as he passes with his barrow, tells him that had his hands been free he would have punched his nose. Because he is different from them, the miners play a cruel, painful trick on him; he cries out in protest and they shamefacedly excuse themselves on the grounds that their life of inhuman toil has deprived them of ordinary human decency. As Gorky walks away along the shore, he feels great sorrow 'at something'—that people should suffer such hardship in life that they regard all others as their natural enemies.

This story reflects the youthful Gorky's desperate search for comradeship. Hungry and destitute he feels himself to be closely linked with the suffering miners, but they reject him because of his superior learning. This personal theme has an underlying national significance—the miners' cruel treatment of the wandering intellectual reflects the hostile reception given by the Russian peasantry to the Populist revolutionaries who came to the countryside to enlighten them. The ability to write up a personal experience in such a way that the story based upon it acquired significance within the context of the life of the whole Russian nation was one of Gorky's outstanding qualities as a writer of short stories.

The story 'My Fellow-Traveller' is based upon a long journey on foot, from Odessa to Tiflis, which Gorky made in August–November 1891 in the company of a Georgian youth named Tsulukidze. In the story Tsulukidze appears as Shakro Ptadze a nineteen-year-old Georgian princeling whom Gorky meets on the docks at Odessa, destitute and starving, and escorts safely to his home in Tiflis, working on the way to obtain food for him and seeing him safely through every danger which they meet during the journey. Gorky presents himself in this story as the exemplary man of action who not only fends successfully for himself in difficult circumstances but provides also for his weaker 'fellow-traveller'. This, however, is not all. Despite his essential helplessness Ptadze professes Chudra's simple, amoral philosophy—'the clever ones grab what's going, the rest get nothing'—and during their short acquaintance the narrator makes strenuous efforts, supported by the example of his own behaviour, to convince him that this outlook contradicts the fundamental obligation of every human being to care about the fate of his fellow-creatures. The narrator is unsuccessful in this but he emerges as the most admirable figure in all of Gorky's early work—an idealistic intellectual who is not only at the same time a man of action but whose deeds conform with his words. Ptadze, on the other hand represents himself as a ruthless, self-reliant, resourceful person, but in action he is cowardly, treacherous, and naïve. The courage and love of adventure which distinguish the predatory Chelkash belong in this story to the narrator, who, however, unlike Chelkash, believes in the moral law and loves work. At the end of the story Gorky writes philosophically that although Ptadze behaved in an unscrupulous manner, he nevertheless remembers him with good-natured tolerance because 'he taught me a lot about a certain view of life'. In 'My Fellow-Traveller' Gorky tells us that the amoral, egocentric outlook which a man acquires when life for him is predominantly a struggle for survival may well conceal inability to cope with adversity. He knew this from personal experience, because many of the predatory merchants of his acquaintance (including his grandfather Kashirin) became victims of the law of the survival of the fittest in which in their prosperous days they implicitly believed. Kashirin's wife, Akulina, a meek selfless woman, fended for him as Gorky fends for Ptadze.

In this story Gorky again invests a personal experience with national significance. The narrator's combination of high moral values with capacity for action marks him as a type of person of whom in Gorky's view late nineteenth-century Russia was sorely in need. It is striking that Gorky should present himself as the positive character needed in Russian life. All of Gorky's self-portraits in his fictional work are somewhat idealized.

Shakro Ptadze, belongs to the band of Gorky's superficially strong men whose strength is illusory when put to the test. In view of the general tendency of nineteenth-century Russian writers to show the strength of the harmonious personality in women but not in men, it is significant that the only Gorkian devotee of Chudra's philosophy who betrays no weakness is a woman—Varenka Olesova, the heroine of the story of that name (1898). Varenka is the daughter of a decayed Russian nobleman, and her outlook is essentially the same as Ptadze's, but whereas the latter is contrasted to his disadvantage with an honest, generous, resourceful man of action, Varenka is depicted favourably by comparison with the hypocritical, prurient intellectual, Sergei Polkanov who deceives himself that he wishes to improve her mind when in fact he desires her body. The final scene of the story, when Polkanov, by accident, comes upon Varenka bathing in the nude and tries to seduce her, unmasks him before himself and before the reader. Varenka treats him with amused contempt. This scene, which is a dramatic confrontation of two people in which the true value of each is revealed, after a story the theme of which has been to contrast them through a close if short relationship, is reminiscent of the closing scene of 'Chelkash'. Both stories illustrate one of Gorky's favourite techniques—the evaluation of human character through a clash between two sharply contrasted people. This technique reflects Gorky's tendency to see moral issues in terms of black and white.

From his great nineteenth-century predecessors Maxim

Gorky inherited interest not only in exceptional strength
but also in abject weakness. His particular view of the
nature of strength and weakness, and of their interrelation-
ship in life, was based upon the fact that he grew up among
people for whom existence was a merciless struggle for
survival. In this world strong men were admired, envied,
and feared and weak men despised and crushed. Compassion was unknown. In his youth Gorky was strongly influenced by this Nietzscheanism of the gutter, and even
though more mature thought and acquaintance with good
books slowly persuaded him that it was wrong, he retained
a certain degree of sympathy for it until about his thirtieth
year. This sympathy is clearly revealed in the fine story
'Kain and Artyom' (1899).

'Every corner of life has its despot'—says Gorky in 'Kain
and Artyom'. The despot of the urban slum in which this
story is set is Artyom, a young ex-peasant of gigantic size;
in this man, employing his favourite device of symbolic
characterization, Gorky embodies his concept of the crude
strength which dominated the life of the lowest strata of
Russian society, as he had known it. There are other ruffians
of great physical strength in the slum, but Artyom's
strength is legendary and he despises and bullies them all.
They, in return, hate him.

In the same slum lives a little Jewish pedlar, Kain, in
whom, in contrast to the mighty Artyom, Gorky embodies
his concept of extreme weakness. This pedlar is an outcast
among outcasts—originally named Khaim (a true Jewish
name and often applied in the plural in Russia to all Jews)
he had abjured his faith and had thus been dubbed Kain
by his fellow-Jews. He is mocked and derided by everyone
around him, even the children.

Artyom, when the occasion arises, bullies Kain unmerci-
fully, but no more so than all the other inhabitants of the
slum, large or small. The pathetic little pedlar feels a strange
sense of gratitude to the giant because he is the only man

he knows who does not discriminate against him but treats him with the same contempt as he shows towards all ordinary mortals. The ruffians of the slum constantly seek an opportunity to avenge themselves upon Artyom for the many hidings he has given them, and one day a group of them come upon him lying helplessly drunk, assault him, and leave him for dead. Kain discovers him, tends his wounds, and implores him in return for protection against his tormentors. For a short while Artyom acts as his defender, but he soon tires of this unaccustomed rôle and abandons the pitiful little Jew once more to persecution.

Gorky delivers no moral judgement upon any of the characters in this story—the superhuman Artyom, the average slum bully, or the cringing pedlar. He shows simply that where life is a struggle for survival everyone must look after himself—the weak can expect no protection from the strong and even the strongest, like Artyom, may be destroyed if they relax their vigilance. This sphere of life is purely and simply a jungle, and Artyom's short period of patronage of Kain springs not from a human sense of moral obligation but from the same kind of instinctive gratitude which an animal might feel for someone who relieved the pain of its wounds. Its gratitude passes with the memory of its pain.

The lesson of the events of 'Kain and Artyom' is that strength owes weakness no automatic debt of protection. The embarrassment which Artyom shows when he is seen in public with Kain indicates, indeed, that strong men may justifiably feel offended at the existence of pitifully weak human beings who claim kinship with them. Gorky tells us in *My Apprenticeship* of the disgust which as a healthy boy he felt at the sight of a crippled girl's deformed body. In the story 'On a Raft' (1895), he shows how a strong, virile merchant, Silan Petrov, having stolen the wife of his impotent son, Misha, blames Misha's impotence for the fact that a man of his social standing finds himself in such an embarrassing position. Russian writers before Gorky, as well as invoking their readers' compassion for weakness, had admired strength if it was directed against falsity or triviality in social life. In certain moods, up to the end of the first decade of his literary career, Gorky is prone to admire strength for no other reason than that it exists. In a story entitled 'The Mistake' (1895), he writes of a blacksmith, Matvei, who coming upon an injured calf beat it to death with an iron bar: 'See how compassionate this Matvei was. He might have done the same thing to a hopelessly sick human being. Is this moral or immoral? No matter, it is strong, and that is the important thing.' Revising this story in the year 1903 Gorky deleted the last sentence, showing thus that he realized that his harsh youthful experiences had made him, in his first years of authorship, show too unconcealed a respect for naked strength. The influence of Nietzsche's writings upon this early life-philosophy is very doubtful—Gorky knew *Thus Spake Zarathustra*, but it is probable that his personal experiences in youth taught him more about selective survival than he could have learnt from any book.

'Kain and Artyom' and 'On a Raft' reveal one side of Maxim Gorky's attitude to strength and weakness as it developed during his formative years spent in the lowest strata of Russian society—great tolerance, bordering on downright admiration, for strength, whatever its misdeeds; and indifference, bordering on contempt, for weakness, whatever its suffering. The fact, however, that in certain youthful moods he was prone to despise the weak and the down-trodden, an outlook unique among major Russian writers, did not prevent him, at other times, from feeling for them the traditional Russian compassion. His sporadic upsurges of contempt for them sprang from his inborn conviction, inherited from both sides of his family and reinforced by experience, that everyone should be able to look after themselves; his pity was rooted in the intensity of his own suffering. 'It was as though the skin had been torn from my heart, making it unbearably sensitive to every injury, my own or another's.' With time, he came to feel only compassion for suffering humanity, but he never lost a strong inclination to seize feckless people by the scruff of the neck and force them to stand up for themselves. In several stories written during the eighteen-nineties, Gorky communicates to the reader his profound compassion for the pitiful beings of whom he writes in them. In the stories 'He Ran Off' (1893) and 'Out of Boredom'(1897) he describes how two lonely, deprived people are reduced to such despair by the cruelty and indifference of their fellow-beings that they commit suicide. In 'He Ran Off' the gaol-bird Ryzhik is committed to hospital with typhus, but none of his friends visit him there; when he comes out he is picked up in a state of destitution by his old criminal accomplice, Saveli, who is now a policeman. Despite their old friendship Saveli refuses to let him go. Ryzhik discovers that Saveli has taken possession of the only companion he had, his dog Gulyai. Overcome by a crushing sense of complete isolation he tears himself free from Saveli, runs off, and drowns himself. In 'Out of Boredom' the tedium of life in a small wayside railway station makes a pointsman, Gomozov, embark upon a love affair with the station cook, Arina, an ill-favoured woman of forty who has never before known love or friendship; also out of boredom the rest of the station staff amuse themselves by subjecting the couple to derision, and Gomozov promptly brings the affair to an end. Humiliated and ashamed Arina runs off into the surrounding steppe from where, when evening falls, she hears the station employees discussing with ribald humour the short affectionate relationship with another human being which had meant so much to her. She comes back to the station and hangs herself.

Ryzhik and Arina are two of the most pitiable creatures in the whole of Russian literature. The source of their suffering is agonizing loneliness—no one thinks for a moment that, abject and friendless though they are, they possess ordinary human sensitivity. In Gorky's merciless world there is no Gogolian clerk to be disturbed for the rest of his life at the thought that the lowliest of his acquaintances is his brother. The most touching characteristic of Ryzhik and Arina is their muteness. They say nothing of the intensity of their suffering until they deliver themselves from it through suicide. This is because they feel there is no one to listen.

In the stories 'Boles' (1897) and 'Twenty-six Men and a Girl' (1899), Gorky deals with one of his most typical and fruitful creative ideas—can men live destitute and friendless lives without comforting illusions to sustain them? As he writes in 'Boles': 'The more bitterness a man has known, the more passionate his longing for something sweet.' In 'Boles', a prostitute, Teresa, asks a student to write letters for her to her fiancé, Boleslav Kashput; a fortnight later she asks him to write one from Boleslav to her; the student realizes that Boleslav does not exist. 'I suddenly understood ... I felt so wretched, so disgusted, so ashamed at something. Three steps from me lives a person without anyone in the world to treat her affectionately or tenderly, and this person invents a friend.' Despite the fact that the student has discovered her secret, Teresa begs him to continue writing the letters and, in return, she darns his clothes and socks. She will not part with her illusion.

In 'Twenty-six Men and a Girl' Gorky describes how twenty-six men, working in inhuman conditions in an underground bakery, find their only ray of consolation in a pretty young serving-girl who comes to the bakery every morning for cracknels. All that their wretched life has left in them of true humanity finds expression in their love for this girl. One day a swashbuckling ex-soldier arrives to work in another part of the bakery; he is very proud of his success with women and boasts to the bakers that he will in a given time seduce their favourite, Tanya. The bakers take a bet with him that he will fail in his plan but on the last day of the agreed period he succeeds. The bakers shout and jeer at their fallen idol. She howls back at them in contemptuous anger because she imagines they are moved by jealousy; she does not realize that they have been deprived of their only illusion. Their desolate life goes on, but now without even the pretence that somewhere something better exists.

'Twenty-six Men and a Girl' is a dramatization of a personal theme of Gorky's life. Seeing around him in youth so much filth, brutality, and human degradation, he seized avidly upon every scrap of evidence that came his way of the existence of something better than the average. He was particularly prone to idealize women. In *My Apprenticeship* he describes his short friendship with a captivating *demimondaine* who came to live in the apartment below that of his relatives, the Sergeevs; her beauty, arrogance, and contempt for the opinions of others delighted her young admirer because they contrasted so sharply with the greyness, joylessness, and hypocrisy of the Sergeevs' way of life, and he applied to her in his imagination the name of the most beautiful woman of whom he had ever read— Queen Margot, the wife of Henry IV of France. One day, however, he visited her apartment, found her with her lover, and realized bitterly that his imaginary queen indulged in the same kind of physical love as the washerwomen who lived near by; he walked sadly home. 'I felt that I had lost something, and for several days I was profoundly unhappy.' The underground bakery described by Gorky in this story is modelled upon Semyonov's bakery in which he worked for a while in Kazan, the sufferings of the twenty-six bakers are based upon those of his real-life comrades there, and in all probability he knew a soldier who won a bet with the bakers that he would seduce a serving-girl in a given time. The bakers' idealization of Tanya and their subsequent disillusionment, however, are fictional, invented

by Gorky to express in dramatic concentration the recurring moods of bitter disappointment which he experienced
in youth because human beings persistently fell short of his
idealistic expectations of them. Gorky communicates to
his readers the intensity of his personal feelings through
showing them as shared by a whole group of twenty-six
men.

Of the major Russian writers only Dostoevsky from personal experience knew as well as Gorky of what extremes
of vice and bestial behaviour lower-class Russian people in
the nineteenth century were capable. Their experience did
not destroy in either writer their natural love for their compatriots, but made them both desperately anxious to discover
among them signs of noble qualities of character or some
evidence of capacity for praiseworthy actions. In their stories
both writers delight in showing such actions whenever
the opportunity arises and in pointing the contrast between
them and the ignoble people who perform them. The difference in their respective outlooks, however, reveals itself in
the fact that Dostoevsky looks only for the traditional Christian qualities of love and compassion, whereas Gorky,
although he does not completely ignore these qualities,
values more highly the virtues of energy, enterprise, and
courage. In the story 'Vanka Mazin' (1897) he describes
how Mazin, an ex-peasant builder's labourer, scales scaffold-
ing on the point of collapse to bring down to safety the
contractor, Zakhar Kolobov; and in 'Kirilka' (1898) he
shows how Kirilka, a peasant acting as ferryman, spends
four hours in the water on an autumn night to save the lives
of six passengers from an upturned boat. The bizarre appearance of these two men contrasts strangely with the
heroism of their actions: Mazin—'A pressed-in, elongated
skull with large protruding ears, a yellow, apathetic face
with tufts of sandy hair on the cheek-bones and the sharp
chin, prominent, colourless eyes, a long nose, a drooping
lower lip and a large, always half-open mouth; a long neck,

covered with knotted veins, sagging shoulders, a hollow chest, a pot belly like a pregnant woman's, the left arm shorter than the right and the legs hooped like a wheel'; Kirilka—'An undersized bandy-legged peasant in a torn, tightly belted sheep skin coat, bent like a bow . . . a little wrinkled face adorned with a sparse grey beard, eyes concealed in bags of wrinkles, thin lips twisted in a smile combining ironical politeness and rascally stupidity.' Such human caricatures as Mazin and Kirilka, strikingly described, abound in Gorky's work. Sometimes the characters of such people belie their unprepossessing appearance, in other cases an ugly exterior clothes an evil or perverted nature. Everywhere in his work Gorky wishes the reader to receive the impression that ugliness, whether physical or spiritual, is part of the mutilation suffered by the Russian people in the course of their tortured history.

The figure of Kirilka was suggested to Gorky by the hero of Korolenko's story, 'The Sportive River' (1891), Tyulin, also a peasant working as a ferryman. Tyulin is crafty, humorous, courageous, and resourceful, and Gorky much admired him as a literary character because he offered a sharp contrast to the figure of the patient, long-suffering Russian peasant much favoured by nineteenth-century writers and typified, in particular, by Tolstoy's Platon Karataev.

Just as in Kirilka Gorky brings forward a fictional peasant whom the reader could set against the Tolstoyan Karataev, so in Natasha, the central character of his story 'One Autumn Evening' (1895), he depicts a prostitute who, unlike Dostoevsky's saintly Sonya Marmeladova, complains bitterly about her treatment by life. 'What blackguards all you men are' declares Natasha. 'I'd like to trample on you, I'd like to maim you! If one of you was croaking, I'd spit in his mug without pity.' Yet this same vituperative girl comforts and shields from the rain with her body the wretched youth who spends the night with her under an upturned boat.

Few writers have refrained from idealizing prostitutes in one way or another—Gorky was no exception.

5

We have seen that one of the aspects of contemporary life with which Gorky was most preoccupied was the disintegration of the human personality, once whole and heroic, into the divided nature of the petty *bourgeois*, in his view the predominant type of late nineteenth- and early twentieth-century European society. We have seen also that the most serious split in the nature of contemporary man, in Gorky's view, was that between his reason and his will—the fundamental defect in the personality of Dostoevsky's Underground Man whom Gorky saw as a special kind of disillusioned, defeated, and embittered petty *bourgeois*. Returning in the early nineteen-twenties to the short-story form Gorky makes striking artistic use of the theme of the divided personality in his tale 'Karamora' (1924).

'Karamora' is the nickname of the petty *bourgeois* Pyotr Karazin, the son of a prosperous locksmith, who in the years before the revolution of 1905 joins the revolutionary movement, but after its defeat allows himself to be suborned into becoming a police spy. After the Bolshevik seizure of power in 1917 he is arrested, and Gorky's story consists of his personal analysis of the reasons for his earlier behaviour, written while he sits in jail awaiting execution.

Karamora's short-lived career as a revolutionary was wholly inspired by his intellectual attachment to socialistic theories. He found such theories not only attractive but also useful because he enjoyed exercising power over other men, and he found that idealistic revolutionaries' acceptance of certain ideas made them easier to command. He regarded terms of imprisonment as useful weapons with which to increase his prestige with his comrades and thus to enlarge his authority over them. The revolution thus meant for him only the indulgence of his petty *bourgeois* ego.

Looking back upon his life, Karamora sees that total devotion to the revolutionary cause on his part could only have sprung from a combination of intellectual conviction and the emotional dynamic which the finest revolutionaries draw from burning love of mankind and hatred of injustice and inequality. Such a dynamic would have given him the will-power to continue to serve the cause in difficult circumstances which love of socialistic ratiocination did not give. Lacking the true conviction which is based upon the co-ordination of reason and emotion he agreed in 1908 to desert the revolution and serve as a police informer. By doing so he avoided punishment for his murder of an ex-comrade who had also turned spy.

Just as Karamora found no moral satisfaction in serving the cause of revolution, so he feels no repugnance at the treacherous nature of his new work. Having found it necessary to change sides in order to save his own life, he carries out his duties in a matter-of-fact manner undisturbed by remorse. 'I betrayed to the police and sent to hard labour one of my best friends, a man of rare moral integrity. I had great respect for his character, his indefatigable spirit, his energy, his good humour and his gay disposition. He had just escaped from prison and gone into hiding for the third time. I betrayed him and waited for something to stir in my soul. Nothing did.' Karamora's mind tells him that his actions are loathsome, but his conscience makes no protest, so he pursues his evil path. From time to time he contrives the escape of some of his former revolutionary comrades, but he does this only for cynical amusement—the whole momentous issue of revolution versus autocracy has no meaning for him except in so far as it allows him to indulge his frivolous, amoral soul.

Gorky's first story to show Dostoevskian influence was 'The Coachman' ('Izvozchik'), written in 1895; the fact that he still found creative inspiration in his great predecessor thirty years later shows the intensity and permanence of his

preoccupation with Dostoevskian thought and psychology.
Defection from the cause of the revolution to the ranks
of police informers was a widespread phenomenon of
Russian political life during the years from 1907–12—
Gorky in 'Karamora' typically attempts to explain this
phenomenon in terms of the psychology of Dostoevsky's
Underground Man. In Dostoevsky's hero, we recall, there
are profoundly tragic elements which Gorky deplored because they seemed to him to represent a romanticization of
the essentially petty *bourgeois* nature of the young men in
real life upon whom the Underground Man was based—
prosaic individualists. In accordance with this view
Gorky in Karamora sets out to debunk the famous Dostoevskian character by presenting him as an undramatic
nonentity whose every action is conditioned by self-interest
—as opposed to Dostoevsky's concept of a being in whom
powerful forces of good and evil fight for predominance.
Dostoevsky presents the vileness of his Underground Man
as a manifestation of the primordial urge towards evil which
he regards as a fundamental part of human nature: Gorky
thought this view metaphysical nonsense, and he exposes
it in 'Karamora' to the ridicule of parody. 'There are various
theories of goodness', writes Karamora: 'the Scriptures,
the Koran, the Talmud, various other books. There must
also be a theory of meanness, of evil. There surely *must* be
such a theory. Everything *must* be explained, everything,
otherwise—how can one live?'

The explanation of Karazin's evil deeds (much fouler,
be it noted, than any committed by the Underground Man),
in Gorky's view, is simple—they spring not from a demonic
principle but from a moral void in his nature; this void has
arisen because petty *bourgeois* concentration on self-interest
has made him incapable of distinguishing between right
and wrong. When circumstances make it necessary he is
capable of anything.

Gorky's identification of his concept of the petty *bour-*

geois with Dostoevsky's Underground Man was an idea full of creative possibilities. The story 'Karamora' is his best artistic treatment of this identification. As always happens, a persuasive work of art does more to convince the reader than pages of argument.

In Karazin Gorky shows a man of petty *bourgeois* origin with a typical petty *bourgeois* personality—egotistical and incapable of emotional involvement. The central character of another story written in the early nineteen-twenties, 'A Tale of Unrequited Love' (1923), is Pyotr Torsuev, the elder son of a soap-manufacturer; of petty *bourgeois* family Torsuev nevertheless shows himself capable of absolute devotion to another human being—he sacrifices the best years of his life to his passionate but unrequited love for a beautiful but untalented actress Larissa Dobrynina. The contrast between Torsuev's social background and his personality enhances his merit as a human being, 'originals'— as Gorky writes— 'are the salt of the earth'.

Of this story the critic Shklovsky wrote: 'The writer has taken an everyday theme of a striking actress with whom a simple, ordinary man falls in love; but as the story progresses, the man grows in stature and the woman becomes ordinary.' Before Torsuev meets Dobrynina he shows little sign of the capacity for devotion which his nature contains— his attachment to his younger brother Kolya, for example, is largely inspired by his estimate of Kolya's value to the business. In a moment of caprice Dobrynina asks him to rid himself of his business in order to devote himself wholly to her—Torsuev does this and from the moment he renounces his commercial responsibility his personality gains in stature in the reader's eyes despite the fact that he has apparently sacrificed material affluence in order to squander his life upon a passion which can bring him only humiliation. Time after time Dobrynina humiliates him both in private and before others, but his devotion is stronger than his self-esteem and he remains her faithful companion until her death at the age of 44, from heart disease brought on by riotous living. He tells his tale to the narrator of the story nine years after her death when he is living on his memories of his beloved in a dark run-down shop in a back street. The once prosperous merchant approaches the end of his life as a poverty-stricken petty tradesman—but his destiny has been fulfilled because his relationship with Dobrynina had given him the opportunity to display the fine devotional power of his nature. Because he feels this sense of fulfilment he refuses to complain.

Dobrynina is a trivial woman unworthy of Torsuev's great love. Her consuming ambition is to win recognition as a great actress but she never rises higher than provincial theatres and all the applause she receives is for her beauty not for her talent; as she loses her beauty with the years audiences humiliate her and in despair she takes to the life of debauchery which eventually precipitates her death. Throughout, Torsuev is aware that she lacks talent but he is indifferent to the theatre and would gladly have seen her leave it. The glamour of the stage which obsesses her plays no part in Torsuev's love. Torsuev knows fulfilment, she only frustration.

This tale is one of Gorky's best. It is fundamentally the story of two people's entire lives which are linked by the love of the one for the other. Nowhere in his work did Gorky show greater skill in psychological analysis; none of his stories is better constructed.

3. THE NOVEL

I

GORKY'S first attempt at a novel, *Paul the Wretched*, was published in twenty-five instalments in the Nizhny Novgorod newspaper *Volgar* between 8 April and 6 July 1894. It is the story of the life of an orphan, Pavel Gibly, from his birth to his imprisonment for the murder of the prostitute Natalya Krivtsova with whom he is in love. Gibly's loneliness in childhood makes him inarticulate and withdrawn, but he has a compelling need to love someone and to be loved in return; before he meets Krivtsova, however, every attempt he makes to establish an affectionate relationship with another human being is brutally rebuffed, and he retreats completely into himself. As a prostitute, Krivtsova is an outcast. When they fall in love these two lonely people dimly glimpse the prospect of happiness and emotional fulfilment in life together; but they have both been so irredeemably spoiled as human beings by their past experience that they are unable to develop their relationship beyond a certain point. Krivtsova thinks that Gibly will be like all other men she has known and that his love for her will die with physical satiation; Gibly, for his part, cannot make himself into the gay, responsive companion whom she desires as a husband. They gradually drift apart and Krivtsova returns to her old sordid existence. Rather than abandon her to other men, Gibly murders her.

Throughout his early life Pavel Gibly feels a growing sense of resentment at something which he cannot define but which prevents him from living in a manner appropriate to his dignity as a human being. This vague enemy finally assumes concrete reality for him as the malevolent force which has made an incorrigible prostitute of the only woman who has ever shown him true compassion and affection. His murder of Krivtsova is the violent expression of the accumulated bitterness of all his previous existence. It is a tragic act because in performing it Gibly destroys not only another person but also his own emotional life. This early work establishes the pattern for almost all of Gorky's subsequent attempts to write a novel. This pattern is the story of a man's life from his birth either to his death or to the occurrence of a catastrophe which brings about the destruction of his inner life. There is an obvious resemblance between the pattern of such works and that of Gorky's own autobiography, with the striking difference that Alexei Peshkov survives the trials and vicissitudes of his youth and early manhood and emerges triumphantly as Maxim Gorky the eminent writer. We should remember, however, that but for a fortunate chance and a surgeon's skill, his life would have ended abruptly by his own hand in Kazan, when at the age of nineteen he made a determined attempt to shoot himself.

Gorky's second novel, *Foma Gordeev*, was published in the Marxist monthly, *Life*, issues 2–4 and 6–9, 1899. The central character of this work is Foma Gordeev, the idolized only son of Ignat Gordeev, a wealthy merchant living in one of the large commercial towns on the river Volga. The narrative follows the general pattern of the earlier novel, tracing the story of the hero's life from birth to an emotional crisis in early manhood which destroys his inner world. In each case this crisis is the culminating point of the hero's conflict with his surroundings which begins in youth and gains in intensity until it erupts, in Gibly's case, in the murder of his mistress, and in Gordeev's in an impassioned speech of moral condemnation of his fellow-merchants. Gibly is a rebel from the lowest sphere of social life and he is condemned to penal servitude for his crime by rich and powerful men of Gordeev's class. Gordeev, however, revolts against the commercial establishment of his town from within and for his act of moral rebellion he is punished more cruelly than is Gibly for his transgression of the law; Foma is declared insane and confined in a lunatic asylum whence, after several years, he returns to his native town truly demented through association with the mentally sick.

In his short stories 'On a Raft' (1895) and 'A Fit of the Blues' (1896) Gorky depicts the merchants Silan Petrov and Tikhon Pavlovich within the limits of a single incident which reveals how they think and act in a specific set of circumstances. In Ignat Gordeev, Foma's father, he draws a finished portrait of the type of boisterous, dynamic businessman of whom Petrov and Pavlovich were preliminary sketches. Ignat is the most sympathetic character in the whole of Gorky's early work, a true son of the writer's native region, the middle Volga, vital, creative, generous, and resolute. Gorky invests his hero with all the affection and admiration which he felt for men like him in real life, men whose commercial achievement delighted and flattered his regional compatriots. Of peasant origin, through hard work and determination Ignat advances from being a barge-hauler on the Volga to wealth and social standing as a barge-owner. The inspiration of his commercial activity is not love of money but the seething energy of his nature. He loves the mighty river because his dynamic personality responds vitally to its elemental strength; one day (indifferent to the financial loss involved) he watches with delight as its swirling waters break up one of his heavily laden barges. Although he is proud of the power he derives from his successful business, his freedom-loving rustic nature resents the possibility that he might become its slave instead of its master. For this reason, when spring brings the renewal of natural life, he abandons all commercial activity and breaks out in a prolonged spell of unbridled debauchery, simply to prove to himself that work has not devitalized him.

In the town where he lives and carries on his business

Ignat Gordeev's greatest friend is another merchant, Yakov
Mayakin, the owner of a rope works. The difference between
the two is that Ignat is a self-made man whereas Mayakin's
family have been successful business men since Catherine's
time. Mayakin's personality shows characteristic traits of
the traditional Russian merchant whose outlook and way
of life are described in the sixteenth-century manual of
family behaviour, *Domostroy*; he admires the teaching of
the prophet Job, regards himself as a divinely appointed
dictator within his family circle, despises women except as
child-bearers, and looks upon commerce as a test of strength
and cunning in which all means of combat are fair and law-
ful. With these historic features, in the composition of
Mayakin's personality, Gorky links certain Nietzschean
characteristics which were widespread among Russian
capitalists of the late nineteenth century—he regards will-
power as the greatest of virtues, thinks of the strong man
as him in whom will-power is harmoniously combined with
intelligence, and abhors the restrictive force of the law
which prevents such men from achieving their purposes.
Gorky involuntarily respects this rigidly authoritarian merchant because he represents an active social force, but at the
same time he hates his contempt for the rights of the free
human personality and loathes his ambition to create a
Russian state based upon the model of a sixteenth-century
Muscovite mercantile family, in which no one dared to
move a finger without paternal permission. Inordinately
proud of his family's past, Mayakin at the same time looks
hopefully to the future when, he is confident, the commercial classes will seize absolute power in Russia. When this
happens, he boasts, they will rule with a rod of iron.

The figures of Ignat Gordeev and Yakov Mayakin are
two of Gorky's greatest artistic creations, forerunners in
his fictional world of the infinitely varied gallery of Russian
men and women of all classes whose portraits make his
memoirs works of great truth and interest. Both are at

the same time types and individuals, both are men of their time yet sum up centuries of Russian history. Their attraction as fictional characters lies in the striking contrast which Gorky draws between them as individuals while emphasizing that they are both members of the same social class. Mayakin disapproves of his friend's profligacy with money and of his undisciplined life, but he values highly his energy and resolution as virtues from the common people which reinforce the historic qualities of the merchantry and will help them to achieve political power. Gordeev dislikes the monastic atmosphere of Mayakin's family life, but he admires his intelligence and commercial acumen. In partnership these two men would be a formidable combination.

The action of the novel *Foma Gordeev* is centred upon the relations between the Gordeev and Mayakin families. Before the story opens Mayakin's son Taras has married against his father's will, and for this act of filial disobedience he has been expelled from the family circle. Mayakin conceives the plan of marrying his daughter Lyuba to Ignat's son Foma, hoping in this way to assure the future of his business by uniting at its head his own family virtues with those of the Gordeevs. At first Lyuba is sympathetically inclined towards Foma because, like many girls of her class towards the end of the nineteenth century, she is in rebellion against her father's dictatorial attitude towards her as a woman and she imagines that Foma's restlessness springs from similar irritation with parental authority. It soon emerges, however, that apart from their shared hostility to their surroundings Lyuba and Foma have nothing in common. Lyuba is a devotee of the new Modernist culture, whereas Foma leaves school prematurely and despises all forms of artistic activity. The superficial attraction between them withers quickly when Foma's rebellious spirit begins to find expression in acts of hooliganism about the town. Lyuba cannot reconcile these apparently senseless actions with his eternal talk about the need to discover the meaning and

purpose of life. Realizing that Foma has inherited the restlessness of his father's character without his creative energy,
Mayakin abandons his plan of making him his son-in-law
and replaces him with Afrikan Smolin, a friend of his son
Taras and the same kind of modern Westernized Russian
businessman. Lyuba accedes to her father's wish that she
marry Smolin, thus bringing to an end her short period of
revolt against his authority. Their marriage unites the traditional merchantry with the sophisticated protagonists of
the Russian industrial revolution. Taras and his father are
reconciled and the unity of the Mayakin family, never
seriously weakened, is thus completely restored. Mayakin's
victory over the dissentient forces within his circle becomes
absolute when he has Foma consigned to a lunatic asylum.

Foma Gordeev's revolt against his own class is complex
and chaotic. It has its roots in nonconformist qualities of
temperament inherited from both his parents. We have seen
that Ignat Gordeev, fearful of becoming the slave instead
of the master of his business, alternates long periods of
devoted work with short bursts of wild living; in his son
this tendency to sporadic fits of rebellion against everyday routine appears as a sustained antipathy to commercial
activity which he regards as prosaic and platitudinous. As
a boy Foma is disappointed to learn that his adored father
is a businessman and not, as he had imagined, a hero of
the folk legends which he delighted in hearing from his
aunt. In youth he shows some interest in the art of managing
men and he is fascinated to discover how readily they obey
an authoritative voice. He is not endowed with great qualities of leadership, however, and he soon comes to regard
the handling of his employees as no less tedious than the
rest of his commercial life.

Foma's mother, Natalya, is his father's second wife, the
first having died from beatings he inflicted upon her because
she bore him four daughters and no sons. She dies in giving
birth to Foma. She is completely different in character from

her husband—a pious Cossack Old Believer, withdrawn, and suspicious of the commercial world into which her marriage has brought her to live. She looks with stern disapproval upon the rich furnishings of her house, because she regards only the inner life as important and material luxury as sinful. Although Foma never knows her, Gorky suggests that he inherits from her a strong tendency to feel at odds with his surroundings. Possibly also one may trace to her his moral condemnation of his fellow-merchants.

Although Foma's reluctance to follow his successful father's path in life may be explained, to a certain extent, by individual characteristics inherited from both his parents, his spiritual malaise reflects a general mood of restlessness and discontent widespread among the sons and daughters of rich Russian businessmen towards the end of the nineteenth century. In his long articles entitled 'Chats about my Craft' (1930–31) Gorky tells us that in the eighteen-eighties and nineties the households of the wealthy merchants of the Volga towns were the scene of bitter conflicts between fathers and children and that the incidence of suicide among the latter was very high. These domestic feuds were a manifestation of the universally disturbed mood of Russian society as the revolution of 1905 drew near, but in individual families they often indicated nothing more serious than a temporary revolt of youth against paternal authority, traditionally despotic in Russian merchant circles. This is the case with the conflict between Mayakin and his son and daughter. Occasionally, however, the causes of strife were more profound, linked with fundamental spiritual or ideological discord, which brought about permanent rifts between the old and the young generations. This is the case with Foma's protest, which is directed not only against his father's desire to make him a merchant against his will but also against the whole new commercial way of life which took shape in Russia in the second half of the nineteenth century. Mayakin is Foma's real enemy, because he aspires

not only to create a commercial empire but also to establish
a social edifice of which, as he typically says, the bricks will
be human beings made to the exact dimensions required by
the master-builder. It is this monstrous vision of the future
which draws from Foma his tortured cry: 'Oh, you swine,
what have you created? Not a new life, not a new social
order, but a prison where you shackle human beings in
chains. It's stifling, cramped, there's nowhere for a living
soul to turn. You destroy the very souls of men.'

We have seen that in 1897 Gorky conceived the idea of
writing a drama about his favourite Russian folk hero, Vasili
Buslaev, the turbulent son of a wealthy merchant of Novgorod the Great, but did not proceed beyond Vasili's boastful opening monologue. The figure of the restless Buslaev
continued, however, to captivate his imagination, and in
his rebellious young merchant Foma Gordeev he eventually realized his desire to show the untamed spirit of his
legendary idol at war with the repressive forces of the
nineteenth-century Russian commercial establishment.
Particularly typical of Buslaev in Gordeev are the acts of
senseless hooliganism which he perpetrates in his native
town because he can think of no better way to express his
hatred of its rulers—one day, for example, he cuts loose a
raft-load of his wealthy friends and sets them adrift on the
Volga because they laugh at the singing of the prostitute
Sasha and the peasant Stepan. Buslaev in the Russian epic
tale is killed when he attempts a feat beyond his powers—
despite repeated warnings he tries to jump longways over
an enormous stone; Gordeev also perishes—spiritually—
because he undertakes an impossible task, the overthrow of
the organized power of Mayakin's commercial world.

Ignat and Foma Gordeev resemble the great River Volga
upon which they live—they are endowed with great
elemental strength which properly channelled can perform
miracles of creative work but frustrated may break out and
cause all manner of destruction. Foma's acts of hooliganism

are the overflow of the dynamic energy which he inherits from his father but for which, unlike his father, he can find no satisfactory outlet; in this respect they resemble Lermontov's hero Pechorin's endless, trivial love affairs, which make him a ridiculous as well as a tragic character. Just as Foma is a son of the Volga, so Pechorin is linked through his name with the Pechora, another Russian river.

One of the great historical tragedies of Russian life, in Gorky's view, was the fact that the enormous natural resources of the country had never been exploited, and that the incomparable elemental strength of the people had never been turned to creative purpose, but expressed itself in daily life in constantly recurring bouts of drunkenness, hooliganism and sexual licence. A spectacle which he occasionally encountered as he wandered through Russia and which gave him great joy was that of gangs of Russian workmen toiling together to carry out some great feat of strength entrusted to them by a merchant or contractor. Such spectacles made him confident that, given the opportunity, the Russian people could make their land a human paradise. In *Foma Gordeev* the result of one of Foma's escapades is that one of his barges sinks to the bottom of the river and he hires a contractor and a team of peasants to raise it. As he watches them at work he experiences the delight which Gorky himself had felt as in real life he watched similar deeds: 'A strange emotion took possession of Foma: he felt a passionate longing to blend with the excited shouts of the workmen, as lusty and as powerful as the river, with the lively splashing of the waves. The perspiration started out on his face from the intensity of his longing and all at once, tearing himself away from the mast, pale with excitement, he rushed with huge strides towards a windlass, shouting in a fierce voice: "All together, now, all together".' This is one of Foma's rare moments of fulfilment in the novel.

Foma Gordeev is a failure as a novel because in it Gorky reduced a theme of great national significance—the conflict of historical forces in a large provincial town on the eve of a great revolution—to the story of one young hooligan's feud with his elders. Although within the confines of a short story Gorky at his best could develop a dramatic situation with great skill, within the longer framework of a novel he could not manage the interrelationships of a group of characters or conduct the unfolding of a series of events. Perhaps the best critical comment upon the artistic defects of *Foma Gordeev* was Gorky's own, made in a letter to the publisher, S. P. Doravatovsky, while he was still writing it: 'Much in it is superfluous and I do not know what to do with the essential and indispensable.' A writer with the natural talent of a novelist allows his work to develop and to take shape according to the demands of the subject he has decided to treat— the subject determines the form; being by nature a writer of dramatic short stories, Gorky was embarrassed by the demands of a broad, complex subject, and in almost every one of his novels he tried to overcome his embarrassment by imposing biographical form upon his material. This method of writing a novel will only be successful if around his chosen hero the writer is able to construct a narrative dealing with all the major aspects of his subject; in the young merchant Foma Gordeev, however, Gorky created a hero who was not typical enough of his kind to stand at the centre of a plot involving the destiny of the whole social class to which he belonged. He is simply one more Gorkian rebel, classless and highly individualized.

Gorky's next novel after *Foma Gordeev* was *The Three of them*, written during the second half of the year 1900 and published in 1901. Gordeev is a rebel from the wealthy mercantile classes who gradually becomes aware of the moral turpitude underlying the impressive façade of the life of his fellow-merchants. The hero of *The Three of Them*, Ilya Lunyev, is a boy who grows up among the filth and brutality of an urban slum, conceives a dream of middle-class respectability as the peak of human happiness, and achieves his dream through successful commercial activity, only to perceive that the social sphere to which he had so fervently aspired is morally corrupt. Thus Gordeev and Lunyev, of different origins, by different routes arrive at the same conclusion.

The story of Ilya Lunyev is something more than the gradual disillusionment of a man with something which, before he possessed it, he imagined would make him happy. Into this basic theme Gorky has interwoven Lunyev's perpetration of a murder, his successful concealment of this murder from the police, and his ultimate confession. Lunyev murders the money-lender Poluetakov, steals 1,850 roubles from his till, and with this money embarks upon a career as a shopkeeper which in time brings him the clean, quiet life of his dreams. Robbery, however, was not the fundamental motive for his crime; he strangled Poluetakov out of an overpowering feeling of disgust at the manner in which he was able to tyrannize over the lives of simple people through the possession of his dishonestly acquired wealth. Lunyev's theft occurs as an afterthought, and he later bitterly regrets that he yielded to the temptation to take the money because by doing so he besmirched the purity of his motive. His feeling of shame and revulsion at having laid the foundations of his prosperity with an evil man's money is much stronger than his remorse for having murdered him.

The 'three' of the title of this novel are Lunyev and his two boyhood friends, Yakov Filimonov and Pavel Grachev, the sons respectively of a publican and a blacksmith. The childhood and youth of these two boys is one long tale of suffering and misfortune, and at the end of the novel Filimonov is dying of consumption and Grachev is ill with venereal disease. Calamity after calamity overtakes them while Lunyev is growing ever more prosperous. The bitter contrast between Lunyev's well-being and the wretchedness of his old friends causes him great anguish and intensifies the discontent which he already feels with his material success through his growing disillusionment with middle-class morality. His spiritual drama, which is the theme of the novel, is made up of the inner conflict which arises in him through the interaction of these two factors. This conflict reaches its climax when he attends the trial of Grachev's mistress, the prostitute Vera Kapitonovna, accused of stealing a merchant's wallet, and finds that the judges are Filimonov's father (who just before had almost beaten his son to death) and other prominent citizens whom he knows to be undetected criminals. From the trial he goes to the house of his shopkeeper friends the Avtonomovs, where a party is in progress; here he publicly denounces the secret infamies of his hosts, then boldly declares himself guilty of his crime. He does this not as the result of torments of conscience but as an act of defiance of the iniquitous society which condones the misdeeds of the wealthy while mercilessly punishing the slightest misdemeanour on the part of the dispossessed. The police are called and pursue him; rather than allow himself to be caught and tried by the infamous judges who tried Kapitonovna he kills himself by running headlong into a wall.

The resemblance of the plot of this novel to that of *Crime and Punishment* attracted the attention of the critics from the time of its publication. Gorky strongly disapproved of the moral influence of Tolstoy and Dostoevsky upon Russian thinkers and writers at the turn of the century, but he himself did not escape their artistic influence. Lunyev and Raskolnikov are similar in that they both commit murder for reasons unconnected with theft and steal during the carrying out of the murder, as it were to rationalize it. Both thereafter feel keener remorse for the theft than for the murder. With Lunyev the money becomes an object of irony because it enables him to achieve the *bourgeois* happiness he wants but comes to despise. This irony increases the agony of his inner crisis and makes him stamp and spit on Poluetakov's grave. Although not an irreligious man (he feels the falsity of his commercial ambitions most intensely in church) he is little troubled by the fact of being a murderer. By confessing to his crime Raskolnikov becomes reconciled with traditional Christian morality and renounces his superman's moral rebellion; Lunyev on the other hand announces his hatred of prevailing social morality by publicly confessing to a crime which flouts it. Raskolnikov is rescued from despair though the example of Sonya's Christian humility. Lunyev, unlike Raskolnikov, remains convinced to the end that his reason for murdering another human being was a good one, but finds himself in an insoluble dilemma because the workings of his social (not his Christian) conscience make him incapable of enjoying the fruits of his crime, whereas his fellow-merchants live happily on the proceeds of every kind of crime, including murder. As well as with Raskolnikov, Lunyev is linked with Pushkin's Herman in the story 'The Queen of Spades'. Before yielding to the temptation of seeking a large fortune through gambling, Herman thinks to himself: 'Prudence, moderation, hard work—these are my certain cards'; Lunyev has similar thoughts at the outset of his commercial career: 'I am literate, intelligent, healthy and hard-working—those are my trump-cards.' Herman abandons his faith in the pedestrian virtues, risks all upon a single card, and loses all he has gained; Lunyev, on the other hand, stubbornly pursues his dream of unspectacular middle-class security. Herman and Lunyev represent different stages in the development of Russian commercial life; the first reflects the psychology of the large-scale capitalist *entrepreneur*, prepared to take big risks for the possibility of great gains, the second is a born shopkeeper, hostile to speculation but content with small profits. The heroic Napoleonic image which inspires the ambitions of both Herman and Raskolnikov is reduced in Lunyev to a dream of petty *bourgeois* happiness.

The trial of Vera Kapitonovna in *The Three of Them* invites comparison with that of Katerina Maslova in

Tolstoy's 'Resurrection', published just before. Both authors pour scorn upon the new judicial system, including trial by jury, created by the Great Reforms, but whereas Tolstoy shows Maslova as the victim of a miscarriage of justice brought about through carelessness on the part of those in charge of the trial, Gorky shows the court as a state institution which supports the evil capitalist society. Tolstoy's judges are immoral, complacent, and irresponsible, but Gorky's are guilty of monstrous, undiscovered crimes. Maslova does not question the authority of the court to try her, although the reader is all the time aware of Tolstoy's conviction that it is wrong for one human being to sit in judgement upon another; Kapitonovna on the other hand does not recognize the legitimacy of the court and rejects the help of her counsel. Maslova's trial first brings home to Nekhlyudov the sinfulness of his early life, and from it his path to resurrection begins; but Kapitonovna's trial brings Lunyov's hatred of *bourgeois* society to its peak and impels him in defiant despair to self-destruction. From the court Nekhlyudov goes straight to the home of his aristocratic friends, the Korchagins, and their way of life seems more discreditable to him than ever before; similarly Lunyev's impassioned denunciation of his *bourgeois* friends, the Avtonomovs, is the immediate consequence of the disgust with which he had just left the court-room. Both Raskolnikov and Nekhlyudov find peace through reconciliation with Christian virtues admired by their creators; for Lunyev there can be no reconciliation because to him, as to Gorky, all life around seems evil and unchanging.

2

Foma Gordeev and *The Three of Them* are literary works which reflect the intense hostility to the Tsarist régime which in differing degrees informed all classes of Russian society prior to the revolution of 1905. Gorky's next novel,

Mother (1906), was written in America after he had left Russia consequent upon the failure of the revolution. This failure produced among artists and thinkers a mood of political despondency which in literature found expression in eroticism, the cult of terror, naturalism, religious questing, and aesthetic experiment. We have seen that the message of Gorky's early stories was directed against the generally bewildered and passive mood of the Russian intelligentsia during the 'eighties, even though by the time he began his career that mood was passing. After 1905 he again planned to use his talent to combat the new predominant mood of political depression, which was more intense than that of twenty years before because it followed a period of almost manic elation. Thus he wrote of his purpose in writing *Mother*—'to sustain the failing spirit of opposition to the dark and threatening forces in life'.

In pursuit of his goal Gorky presents a group of Social Democrat revolutionaries engaged in stimulating peasants and workers to revolt during the years immediately preceding 1905; their confidence in the rightness of their cause and its ultimate triumph, their mutual devotion, their indifference to personal interests contrast sharply with the pessimism, militant individualism, and sensual self-indulgence which Gorky saw as the basic vices of Russian society when the novel was written. Gorky is trying to present them as models of noble behaviour, as during the 'nineties he had brought forward his romantic tramps as the bearers of virtues which in his view contemporary people had lost. Unfortunately, although the virtues with which he endows his revolutionaries were often possessed by their real-life prototypes, he fails to bring them alive. This applies most of all to their leader, Pavel Vlasov. His function in the novel comes to very little more than to proclaim the socialist faith before the judges presiding at the trial of the little group which is the culminating point of the action; this proclamation repeats in political form the moral protests made by

Gordeev and Lunyev. The fact that in *Mother* it is delivered before a court of law, a state institution, gives it revolutionary as well as ethical force.

Mother is proclaimed by Soviet critics as a model of the genre of socialist realism. The only possible justification for such a claim lies in the hatred with which Gorky depicts in it the champions of the old order and the affection which he lavishes upon the revolutionaries. Reality in a work of the school of Socialist realism should be portrayed as revolutionary, that is, orientated towards the future when social institutions and human psychology will have assumed new socialist forms. It is difficult to see such a reality in *Mother*. Both the factory workers and the peasants, to whom the revolutionaries address their summons to rebellion, remain confused and unresponsive. The only person in the novel who develops psychologically is the mother, Pelageya Nilovna Vlasova, who enters the action as a devoted member of the Orthodox Church, the long-suffering widow of a brutish Russian workman, and in the final scene is arrested for distributing revolutionary pamphlets. Her development is not, however, from a religious to a socialistic outlook but from one kind of religious outlook to another, from that which worships God in heaven to that which looks towards the establishment of His kingdom on earth. She at first passively accepts evil as the will of God, but in the course of the action she becomes convinced that she must actively strive to extirpate it; her transformation thus reflects Gorky's favourite contrast in human types, that of the resigned and unrebellious with the dynamic and combative. The chief influence in her psychological development is not the teachings of scientific socialists but the 'God-building' aspirations of the peasant Rybin, who believes that mankind must re-create for themselves the true image of God because the established Church has falsified His nature, presenting Him as the scourge of sinners instead of the source of truth and justice. She finally abandons formal religious practice when in a dream she sees the figure of a priest shouting to the police to take her beloved revolutionaries into custody.

Pavel Vlasov, Pelageya's son, as a youth is coarse and drunken like his father. His interest in the revolutionary movement coincides with the beginnings of improvement in his character, of which the first outward sign is religious in nature—he brings home and hangs in his room a picture of the risen Christ.

In the early drafts of *Mother*, Pelageya Nilovna is about sixty years of age, modelled probably to a certain extent upon Gorky's beloved grandmother; it was only in the last of six versions, prepared in 1922, that she first appeared as a woman of forty. This was a beneficial alteration, because it not only made her psychological transformation more plausible in a younger woman but also enabled the reader to imagine her as still active at the time of the October revolution. In general in the novel Gorky gives his revolutionaries the attraction of youth, whereas the defenders of autocracy are presented as old, yellow-faced, and on the point of extinction. He thus implies that the future lies with the socialist cause. This adulation of youth is somewhat at variance with his practice in his earlier stories in which the most sympathetic characters are usually, like Chelkash and Ignat Gordeev, men of mature years but still strong and virile; young men, like Gavrila and Shakro Ptadze, are often puppy-like and dependent. In presenting Vlasova as a woman of forty he struck a happy balance. Her real-life prototype, Anna Kirillovna Zalomova, was fifty-two at the time of the May Day demonstration in Sormovo in 1902 which inspired the central incident of the novel. She had seven children, including two daughters, whereas Vlasov is Pelageya Nilovna's only child—by making this alteration Gorky intensified the emotional link between the mother and son. Pelageya's motive for her first action in the revolutionary cause is not ideological but maternal—

she agrees to distribute leaflets after Pavel's first imprisonment because if they are not distributed while he is in jail
the police will know that he was guilty of earlier distribu-
tions. Gorky, however, does not successfully develop the
emotional relationship between the two. The reader is left
with the strong impression that Pelageya regards all the
revolutionaries as her children. Her attitude to Rybin and
later to the Dostoevskian misanthrope Vesovshchikov is
warmer than her feelings for the stiff ascetic Pavel.

Gorky's attempt in *Mother* to reconcile in the figure of
Pelageya Nilovna his socialist convictions with the religious
aspirations he acquired in childhood from his grandmother
and never completely lost was a reflection of the religious
preoccupations widespread among the Russian intelligentsia
after the failure of the revolution of 1905. Many Russian
thinkers at this time, convinced of the impossibility of
realizing the kingdom of God on earth, turned their attention to the seemingly more tractable problem of assuring
their personal immortality in heaven. Gorky, however, from
his Italian exile, kept his eyes firmly fixed upon the evils
of this world, as exemplified in Russian reality, and sought
in religious thinking stimulus to revive and sustain the
revolutionary cause at home. We have seen how, when he
left the Kashirins, he came to hate his grandfather's Old
Testament religion of fear and vengeance; and at the same
time became disillusioned with his grandmother's devotion
to the tenets of the Sermon on the Mount. Yet, as Tolstoy
once shrewdly told him, Gorky could not get on without a
God, and this spiritual need asserted itself strongly in his
prevailing mood of dejection after the destruction of the
high revolutionary hopes which he expressed with such
fervour in 'The Song of the Stormy Petrel' (1901). Rejecting
traditional concepts of God which seemed to him either to
sanction repression or to encourage resignation, he began
to look for a new faith which would further the cause of the
Russian revolution while still exalting Christian notions of

freedom and justice. This new quest, which involved a search for suitable men and women to put the faith into practice, replaced after 1905 his earlier attempts to find a strong, individualistic hero. He has left an artistic record of his spiritual seeking during these years in the short novel *Confession*, published in 1908. This novel is linked with his Capri school of the following year (see page 55). The figure of the wanderer-narrator constantly recurs in Gorky's early stories. In some he appears simply as a participant in the action ('In the Steppe', 'The Affair with the Clasps'), in others as a seeker and moralist ('Makar Chudra', 'My Fellow-Traveller', 'Konovalov'). Gorky's physical wanderings are indeed linked with his mental searching, because it was partly spiritual malaise which made him take to the roads. *Confession* is the account of the disillusionment of Matvei, an orphan boy, with traditional Christianity and his subsequent wandering through Russia in search of a new image of God. In describing this boy's physical vagabondage in quest of a spiritual ideal, Gorky is externalizing his own inner seeking.

Matvei, like Gorky, wanders because he is inwardly disturbed. Like his creator, he is greatly troubled by the conditions of human life around him: 'Turbid streams of misery flow everywhere over the face of the earth and I see to my horror that amid all the chaos and strife there is no place for God. There is nowhere where his strength can assert itself, nowhere where it can take root; life, consumed by the worms of grief and fear, malice and despair, greed and shamelessness, disintegrates into ashes, people are destroyed, isolated from each other and disabled by loneliness.' Matvei's feeling that the human wretchedness he sees everywhere denies the existence of God reflects Gorky's mood of rebellion against established religion in 1908. Matvei's shaken faith is finally completely destroyed by two personal catastrophes, the death of his wife in child-birth and the accidental poisoning of Sasha, his first-born son; he sets off to wander about Russia in search of a new deity to replace the traditional Christian God in whom he can no longer believe. This new God must be a force capable of performing the miracle of creating a better life for humanity on earth—a task in which the old God failed. Matvei's search ends successfully in Siberia, where he meets a group of 'Godbuilders'; these men blame for the evil they find in life the predatory self-assertion of aggressive individuals, and they oppose to this evil force the miraculous God-bearing power of the collective will of the people. Returning from Siberia to the province of Kazan, Matvei witnesses a miracle performed by the new divine force he has discovered. An icon is being returned to a monastery from a nearby town and a sick girl is laid at the monastery gates; the crowd following the icon press round her and by the exercise of their collective will make her rise and walk. That night Matvei, sitting alone, feels 'indissolubly linked for ever in spirit with the people' and mentally addresses them: 'You are my God, the creator of all Gods, whom you have fashioned from the splendour of your soul in the toil and trouble of your searching.'

This discovery of God in the Russian people is the successful outcome of Matvei's quest. On the way to Siberia he visits a monastery, where he first hopes to find God, in the place where He might most naturally be expected to be present. Here, however, Matvei encounters only mutilations of the ancient Russian piety. In a coffin, twenty steps beneath the ground, wrapped in a shroud, sits the monk Mardari, counterfeiting death; in a luxuriously furnished cell lives Father Antoni, regularly receiving female visitors and contemptuous of all human beings. Leaving the monastery and looking back upon it, bathed in the beautiful evening light, Matvei thinks: 'Amid this soul-stirring beauty live benighted people, wrapped in long robes; live and rot, passing empty days in meaningless toil, loveless, joyless, surrounded by filth.' By making Matvei first visit this foul monastery Gorky emphasizes the need for a new faith to replace the old which has fallen into such corruption and decay; and he contrasts the morbidity and dissoluteness of monastic life with the fresh creative spirit of the people.

In *Confession* Gorky expresses artistically the same ideas which in the year 1908 he expressed philosophically in his long article 'The Destruction of Personality'—condemnation of the predatory individual who preys upon the masses, and exaltation of the miraculous productive power of the collective strength of humanity. We have already seen how in the novel *Foma Gordeev* Gorky expressed his confidence in the omnipotence of collective effort in everyday affairs in his description of the near-miraculous raising of Gordeev's sunken barge by a group of peasants; the religious, God-building cast of his mind in 1908 finds expression in the fact that in *Confession* the same collective will performs a typical Scriptural miracle.

In each of Gorky's novels so far examined, except *Mother*, the author has based his narrative upon the life story of a single young man. In each case this man's spiritual seeking, which constitutes the theme of the novel, is conditioned by his childhood experiences; Gibly, deprived and lonely, longs for affection and companionship in a fulfilled human relationship, Gordeev, alien to the merchant world in which he grows up, desperately seeks the true meaning and purpose of life, Lunyev, exposed to every kind of cruelty and deprivation, strives to create for himself a clean, well-fed existence, Matvei, disabused of his faith in the Christian God of love, seeks a new God to satisfy the demands of his religious nature. In each one of these novels the hero's life story is followed up to his middle twenties, that is, approximately to the age at which Gorky closes his own autobiography. Each one of them is short. In *The Life of Matvei Kozhemyakin* (1910) Gorky writes a very long novel in which he recounts the life of his hero from birth to his death at the age of about fifty-five. As in earlier works, he begins by relating the formation of a boy's outlook and personality under the influence of his surroundings; Matvei Kozhemyakin grows up in the small provincial town of Okurov, the son of Saveli Kozhemyakin, a self-made merchant in the style of Ignat Gordeev. In this novel, however, it is not Gorky's purpose to describe the inner conflicts of a merchant's son who does not wish to follow a commercial career. His attention is focused rather upon the town of Okurov, the manners and customs of which are the decisive influence upon the formation of his hero's personality. In describing life in Okurov Gorky probably had in mind the town of Arzamas, the largest town in his native region after Nizhny Novgorod itself; but his aim was to create a representative likeness of hundreds of medium-sized provincial Russian towns and to show how these towns moulded the outlook of the people who grew up in them. Gorky believed that the revolution of 1905 had failed fundamentally because the historical experience of the mass of the Russian people had made them incapable of true revolutionary thinking, and in his view the way of life of towns like Okurov had played a decisive part in this experience. In his novel he presents Matvei Kozhemyakin as the heir to the brutality, ignorance, superstition, and indifference which had marked the life of his native town for centuries.

Having described Kozhemyakin's formative years, up to his early twenties, Gorky then moves on to the last twenty years of his hero's life. These years cover roughly the period from the mid eighteen-eighties to 1905, a period during which from their different standpoints Russian radical thinkers were preparing the way for the first revolution. Two such thinkers, Evgeniya Mansurova, a Populist, and Mark Vasilev, a Marxist, returning from Siberian exile, spend some time in Okurov, and Kozhemyakin in his late thirties and forties comes under their influence. Like Foma Gordeev, Matvei is keenly aware of the imperfections of the life of his social class; the issue at stake in his later years is

whether under the influence of advanced political thought
his moral disapproval can be transformed into a true radical
conscience. The influence of Okurov, however, is too strong;
he dimly perceives that standards of behaviour which from
childhood he had accepted as normal are abhorrent to en-
lightened people from outside Okurov, but he lacks the
will-power to change his own pattern of conduct. Thus
when he falls in love with Mansurova and she rejects him,
he tries to rape her. In the same way, towards the end of the
nineteenth century, the Russian people under the influence
of revolutionary thought were aware that great changes
must be made in the government of their country, but they
lacked the spirit of resolution necessary to bring such
changes about. Thus, as the spiritual prisoner of his past,
Kozhemyakin is a symbol of the Russian people as a whole.
He dies on a May morning in 1905, as also in that year the
hopes of the Russian revolutionary movement seemed
to die.

   This novel is the story of a struggle between the forces
of light, represented by Mansurova and Vasilev, and the
forces of darkness, embodied in the life of Okurov, for the
possession of a man's soul. The final result of this struggle
is the total defeat of the forces of light—not only do Mansurova and Vasilev fail to change Kozhemyakin, but
Mansurova's short sojourn in Okurov adversely affects her
sense of revolutionary purpose. When she leaves the town
she becomes an apostle of the non-revolutionary theory of
'small deeds' (see page 15) which was fashionable among
large numbers of the intelligentsia during the eighties and
nineties. The defeat of Gorky's radical thinkers in this novel
by the medieval atmosphere of Russian provincial life (the
Russian people's Asiatic inheritance, insisted the writer)
is as complete as the rout of his rebellious hobos by the
nineteenth-century forces of law and order in his early
stories. Like Dostoevsky, Gorky seeks God but shows the
Devil as the stronger.

3

Gorky's novel *The Artomonov Business* was written in 1924–5 and published in 1925. Like *Foma Gordeev* and *The Life of Matvei Kozhemyakin* this novel depicts, against the mid-century background of ever-quickening commercial activity, the meteoric rise of a business founded by an ex-serf in a stagnant Russian provincial town. Whereas, however, the first of these novels is concerned with the inner life of the central character and the second with the intimate connexion between life in the town and the development of the hero's personality, the basic theme of the later novel, as the title makes clear, is the fate of the business itself. It is founded in 1863 and swept away by the revolution of 1917. During this period three generations of Artomonovs participate in the management of the business (a linen factory). Although the fate of the business (and with it that of Russian capitalism in general) is the basic theme of the novel, Gorky, always predominantly concerned with people, is more interested in the influence which its management exerts upon each member of the family than in the political and economic processes which result in its destruction. Because of the interweaving of the historical theme with personal destinies and the distribution of the narrative interest among three generations instead of its concentration upon one person, Gorky in this work could more justly claim to have written a true novel than in either of the other two.

The founder of the business is Ilya Artomonov, who, freed in 1861, arrives two years later in the small town of Dryomov and sets out to establish there a commercial dynasty and family home. Dryomov is another Okurov; its inhabitants, sunk in medieval sloth, and superstition, resent the intrusion of a dynamic commercial family upon their slumber (the Russian verb 'dremat' means 'to doze') as much as Kozhemyakin's townsmen hate the disruptive ideas of radical thinkers. Whereas, however, the spirit of Okurov overcomes the influence of modern thought, the nineteenth-century energy of Ilya Artomonov quickly enables him to seize economic power in Dryomov. Gorky illustrates the victory of the new over the old in this town through a symbolical relationship between the Artomonov family and that of Evsei Baimakov, the mayor. In order to establish his standing in Dryomov Ilya contrives the marriage of his eldest son, Pyotr, to Baimakov's daughter Natasha; then, when Baimakov very soon dies, Ilya steps into his shoes, first of all by renting the house he had lived in and later by taking his widow, Ulyana, as his mistress. The initial success of the Artomonov business is symbolized in Ilya's taking possession of Baimakov's wife and house; the eventual failure of their children's marriage illustrates the long-term failure of Ilya's plan to found his family's fortunes upon the union of Artomonov energy with Baimakov patriarchal authority. To their marriage Natasha brings only the most backward features of old Russian mentality, and she earns her husband's contempt by remaining afraid to the end of her life of modern inventions such as the gramophone and the sewing-machine.

Ilya Artomonov dies in the very act of establishing his business. The manner of his death symbolizes the degree to which henceforth the business will dominate the destiny of each member of the family; after a night of carousing he joins his workers in an attempt to manhandle a new boiler three hundred and fifty yards from the wharf to the factory, and dies of over-exertion. Thus the founder of the business becomes its first human sacrifice.

Upon Ilya's death the management of the business devolves upon his son Pyotr Artomonov, who is the central character of the novel. Born in 1842, Pyotr spends the first twenty years of his life in the country, and this distinguishes him from Foma Gordeev and Matvei Kozhemyakin, who are townsmen born and bred. Also unlike Foma and Matvei,

Artomonov accepts, although unwillingly, the responsibilities of his commercial inheritance. The tragedy of his life, however, is that the memory of the freedom and peace of his rustic youth never leaves him, and he regards the business as an evil force which has destroyed his hopes of happiness. The conflict within him between the born peasant and the reluctant businessman reaches its climax in a hotel room where he stays on his way home from a bout of debauchery at a fair; looking in the mirror, the businessman sees the tear-stained face of the unhappy peasant, 'the one who was to blame, the one who stopped him from marching through life easily and confidently', and in fury he hurls a bottle at it. In Gorky's short stories we find this same inner conflict in the ex-peasant Artyom, the bully of the urban slum, who vents his bitter regret for the lost rustic happiness of his childhood by breaking out, when his nostalgia becomes unbearable, in bouts of wanton destruction and assault. Many Russian businessmen spent their lives like Pyotr, working, carousing, and squandering money. A long line of peasant ancestors, however, have left in Pyotr a compelling desire to work for a master, and he never develops the mentality of an employer. Uprooted, resentful, at a loss, he is but one of millions of Russian ex-peasants who in the capitalistic society of the late nineteenth century search in vain for the peace they knew in their youth in patriarchal times. The cares of business only increase his wretchedness. His tragic unhappiness is born of the most fertile source of tragedy in human life—loneliness.

In 1902 in the Crimea Gorky mentioned his plan for writing *The Artomonov Business* to Tolstoy, and the latter expressed great interest in the subject, especially in the question of the moral degeneration of the family over three generations; in 1909, on Capri, Gorky told Lenin of his still unrealized project, and Lenin inquired how the writer proposed to end the story and advised him not to write it until the coming revolution provided an ending from reality.

The different reactions of the two great men point an issue fundamental to the whole conception of the novel; is the Artomonov business the victim of history or is the moral decadence of its owners so great that it would have foundered even without the revolution? In Gorky's treatment of his theme the moral and political factors are interlinked, because the approaching holocaust contributes significantly to the spiritual malaise of the family.

Pyotr Artomonov is the only member of the family whose life-span covers the entire period of the existence of the business. Commercial success makes him unhappy but not morally degenerate; in this respect, despite his drunkenness and fornication, he is not inferior to the average run of prosperous businessmen of his acquaintance. Signs of decadence from easy living are, however, clearly visible in his second son, Yakov. Gorky presents Yakov Artomonov as the complete type of the petty *bourgeois* whom he had characterized twenty years earlier in his article 'Notes on the petty bourgeois mentality'. Immoral and purposeless, Yakov longs for social stability so that he may enjoy in peace the comfortable life earned by the hard work of his more energetic relatives. For him the highest peak of human happiness is 'the feeling of satiation excluding all desire'. The threat of revolution unmans him completely. He plans to flee Russia with his mistress Polina, but is beaten up by revolutionaries in a train on the way to Moscow and dies.

The bitterest grief in Pyotr Artomonov's unhappy life is caused by the refusal of his beloved elder son, Ilya, to participate in the management of the business, and his adherence to the revolutionary cause. Ilya leaves Russia and returns only to play his part in the events of 1917. Gorky does not paint a detailed portrait of him, but hints that he has inherited the best qualities of his grandfather—determination, fearlessness, love of the Russian people—and thus implies that the best from Russia's past joins the revolution. Ilya tells his father his reasons for rejecting his commercial inheritance, and in them Pyotr hears 'something which echoed his own confused thoughts'. Pyotr's abhorrence of the enslavement of mankind—both employers and workers—by commerce is the elemental reaction of a peasant accustomed in childhood to rustic freedom; in his son Ilya this elemental hostility becomes reasoned opposition with revolutionary aims. In Gorky's scheme of values this represents advance, not decadence. Ilya, however, is only a presence in the novel, the threat of revolution from abroad, and no more a living character than Gorky's revolutionaries in *Mother* or *Matvei Kozhemyakin*.

For different reasons, then, neither of Pyotr Artomonov's two sons makes any significant contribution to the management of the business, and each in his own way reflects his father's negative attitude to it. The commercial life, however, is markedly more congenial to Pyotr's cousin (and adopted brother) Alexei and his son Miron. Alexei was the illegitimate son of old Ilya's sister and a nobleman. The peasant strain persists in him (as, for example, when he brutally and without cause kills his sister-in-law's pet bear), but the means provided by the successful family business enable him to indulge his inherited nobleman's tastes for luxurious living, and this creates antagonism between him and his boorish brother. At the same time, however, Alexei's naturally lighter and less suspicious attitude to life and people makes him more adept than Pyotr at selling the company's goods. He is also more receptive to new industrial techniques, which Pyotr distrusts out of peasant dislike for every kind of innovation. Because of Pyotr's inability to keep pace with nineteenth-century industrial progress, control of the business, as it grows and flourishes, gradually passes from his hands into those of his brother and nephew. Miron Artomonov differs from his father and grandfather in that he is a modern professional businessman whereas Alexei and old Ilya are, in differing degrees, simply primordial sources of commercial energy. Old Ilya ran the business single-handed but Miron, had he survived, would have required the help of accountants and technicians; this is not because he is a smaller man but because commercial management in his time becomes more complex than in his grandfather's. Had circumstances permitted, there seems little reason to doubt Miron's ability to develop the business into a successful modern concern.

Pyotr Artomonov differs from Alexei not only in his attitude to the business but also in his relationship with his sons. As he talks to Ilya and Yakov it strikes him that he is not for them such a fearsome figure as his father was for him, yet he tries to impose upon them old Ilya's sixteenth-century ideas of parental discipline. Thus, when Ilya expresses a desire to leave home against his father's wishes, and declares that every man has the right to live as he wishes, Pyotr replies that he is not a man but his son; and threatens that when he returns he will be given the most menial tasks to perform. He views with disfavour Miron's habit of talking to his father like an equal and arguing with him as man to man. In the sense that Pyotr can no longer order his sons' lives as his ancestors did, he is inferior to the latter, but his real weakness lies in his failure to see that sixteenth-century methods of domestic control are no longer viable in the mid-nineteenth century. His family unhappiness is rooted in the same mental backwardness as his malaise among businessmen.

Pyotr has a second brother, the hunchbacked Nikita. Old Ilya's plan for him was that he should become a monk and pray for forgiveness for the sins the family were sure to commit in building up the business. Like Matvei in *Confession*, Nikita loses his faith because of the evil he sees in the world, in particular the unmerited early death of his father; yet he still enters a monastery, and thus becomes one of the numerous non-believing monks we find in Gorky's work, through whom he wishes to show the decadence of the old religious spirit in nineteenth-century Russia. Nikita decamps from his monastery.

One of the most typical features of Gorky's literary technique was symbolical characterization. In the short stories perhaps Chelkash is the best example of this art, in the plays Luka in *The Lower Depths*. Highly symbolical in *The Artomonov Business* is the enigmatic figure of Pyotr Artomonov's ditch-digger and odd-job man, Tikhon Vyalov. This patriarchal figure represents the passivity and inertia of old Russian life, in contrast to the nineteenth-century dynamism of the Artomonovs. His names (*tikhi*—quiet, *vyali*—flaccid) suggest his nature. The manner in which he works for Pyotr—as though doing him a favour, aware that he is capable of better things—symbolizes the unwilling participation of the Russian peasantry in urban commercial enterprise. At the same time Vyalov stands for Nemesis, dogging the steps of the Artomonovs from the time of the foundation of the business until its destruction. He is present at every catastrophe which overtakes them. When Nikita comes out of the room where his father has just died, the first man he sees is Vyalov performing the symbolic action of breaking splinters from a piece of wood and one by one stamping them into the sand until they disappear. When Nikita attempts to hang himself after hearing his sister-in-law Natasha, whom he loves, speak contemptuously of him, it is Vyalov who cuts him down. After Pyotr has murdered Pavel Nikonov, a boy for whom he has an obsessive hatred, he looks round and finds Vyalov standing behind him, but cannot make out whether the latter saw the deed or not, and Vyalov does not enlighten him. When Alexei dies of a heart attack, it is Vyalov who brings the news to Pyotr. At one point Pyotr is so exasperated by this man who seems to intrude into every niche of their family life that he sacks him and sends him away, but this is tantamount to trying to escape his destiny, and one year later Vyalov returns. On his return he announces Nikita's flight from the monastery.

When the revolution breaks out it is Vyalov who explains to Pyotr what is happening. Throughout the life of the business Vyalov adopts a proprietorial attitude towards it, watching over it, as it were, in his role of historical representative of the Russian people, against the time when the people will claim it. In the final scene of the novel, as revolutionary disturbances rage outside the house, Vyalov and Pyotr confront each other inside—two old men who have served the business since its foundation—and Vyalov presents to his master the moral reckoning for the sins the family have committed during the fifty-four years of their commercial activity; Gorky deliberately withholds any hint of the dramatic from his indictment and thus emphasizes the view he wishes the reader to accept—that the misdeeds of the Artomonovs have not been greater than those of the average Russian commercial family and that accordingly their disappearance is not a special case. Vyalov's indictment is Christian; the Artomonovs' destroyers are Bolsheviks. They are thus condemned by both the old Russia and the new. With them the whole of Russian capitalism is arraigned at the bar of history.

The theme of *The Artomonov Business* is based upon the ideas Gorky had expressed many years earlier in the articles 'The Destruction of Personality' and 'Notes on the petty bourgeois mentality', and in the novel *Confession*. Gorky wishes us to compare, to their detriment, each succeeding member of the family with old Ilya and to show how each generation, moving further away from the people, diminishes correspondingly in spiritual stature. This progressive estrangement is expressed in the deterioration of relations between the family and their workers. Ilya behaves very simply with them, attends their weddings and christenings, and they regard him as a peasant like themselves only more favoured by fortune. Pyotr is sullen and tyrannical with them because they represent the business cares which have spoilt his life. Alexei, half-nobleman, calls them rogues and ne'er-do-wells and scolds them. Yakov despises the workers, but he is terrified by the ever-growing proletarian movement. Miron understands that they are not concerned merely with obtaining reforms and attempts to win their co-operation by establishing for them libraries and sporting clubs, 'feeding wolves with carrots', as he puts it. Young Ilya, the Marxist, regards them, of course, in a different light from his relatives; in him, the best member of the third generation, old Ilya's oneness with the Russian people is restored, but whereas the commercial path chosen by the latter begins the alienation of the family from their own social class, his grandson's political activity reunites them, at least until the revolution. Gorky presents the short hey-day of Russian capitalism as an aberration in the history of the nation.

Gorky wrote his last novel, *The Life of Klim Samgin*, during the years 1925 to 1936. His purpose in this work was to draw an epic picture of the ideological conflicts among the Russian intelligentsia from the mid eighteen-seventies to the revolution of 1917, and to fit into this picture a con-demnatory portrait of his central character, Klim Samgin, a liberal intellectual. This was a most promising subject for a major novel, and Gorky's work, if successful, would have been a significant contribution to world literature; unfor-tunately it is an abject failure.

In sketches and stories throughout his career Gorky re-morselessly attacked the figure of the liberal intellectual. His most successful creation of this type of person is the hero of the story 'Varenka Olesova', the university lecturer Sergei Polkanov in whose depiction art and didacticism are excellently blended. In the broader framework of a long novel, the action of which extends over a period of forty years, Gorky aimed at presenting a complete picture of the type instead of, as earlier, only a fragmentary sketch. The completeness, however, lies only on the negative side. The lawyer Klim Samgin combines in himself every vice which his creator regarded as typical of petty *bourgeois* psychology. Hedonism, political apathy, self-conceit, hypocrisy, and commercial opportunism are his distinguishing characteristics. Gorky's task was to combine the achievement of his accusatory purpose with the realization of his epic conception; he attempts to do this by showing Samgin's character through his attitude to the major historical events of his time and in his relationships with people who represent its principal ideological trends. Samgin imagines himself to be a man of advanced political views, but he plays only an insignificant part even in the revolutionary events of 1905, which rallied all the progressive sections of the intelligentsia. His participation in these events, however slight, is brought about entirely by accident; he follows a procession of Social Democrats because it is going in the direction of his house, and he becomes involved in street fighting because two barricades are erected where he cannot avoid them leaving or returning home. His true political sympathies are divined by Colonel Vasilev, an officer of the gendarmerie who interrogates him when he is arrested during the disturbances and invites him to turn police informer; to his own astonishment, Samgin is not in the least offended by this proposal. Samgin's astonishment typifies the self-deception which in Gorky's view lay at the basis of the outlook of the liberal intellectual. Gorky paints this self-deception in other ways. Samgin becomes aware, for example, that he is involuntarily attracted to people who actively fight the revolution—the professional spy Mitrofanov and the agent-provocateur Nikonov—and he perceives some of his own characteristics in them. As the revolution approaches Samgin's attitude to it becomes more and more ambiguous until finally he realizes that he detests the thought of it. His life ends when he is *accidentally* killed during the upheaval of 1917—he is not even a convinced defender of Tsarism. Samgin's conservatism is based entirely upon his only strong desires in life—to protect his material prosperity and to absolve himself from the need for facing the fundamental political issues of his time. One of his acquaintances is Dmitri Kutuzov, a Marxist, who like all of Gorky's Marxists expounds his views in a serene, confident voice indicating their unchallengeable correctness; to this man's calm arguments Samgin can think of only one answer, 'I am against it'.

Of Goncharov's Oblomov Chekhov once said that he 'was a character not nearly big enough to make it worth while writing a whole book about him'. This remark, of doubtful truth with regard to Oblomov, pinpoints exactly the reason why Gorky's long novel was foredoomed to failure when he decided to place at its centre such a footling nonentity as Samgin; the length of the work springs not from the significance of its subject but from the fact that the author enjoys venting his hatred on his puppet hero through four considerable volumes. The reader quickly tires of this protracted persecution. In a book of this length one would have expected Gorky to exploit his exceptional gifts of characterization and to compensate to some degree for the insignificance of his central character with a striking gallery of minor figures. Even in this realm, however, he fails utterly. As so often happened with him when he was dealing with members of the intelligentsia, he presents the great body of Samgin's innumerable acquaintances not as people but as vehicles for the expression of political, religious, and aesthetic opinions current during the decades covered by the action of the novel. In striving to impart ideological significance to all their personal relationships he destroys their reality as human beings.

4. MEMOIRS

UP to the year 1911, in twenty years of work, Gorky produced only a few short stories and one play which merit the
name of great literature. This year is noteworthy in his
career because during it he wrote and published (in the
October issue of the magazine *The Contemporary*) his first
literary portrait, a sketch of the Populist writer A. E.
Karonin-Petropavlovsky. Some months later, in the 'Knowledge' miscellany for the year 1912, he published his first
autobiographical memoir, 'An incident from the life of
Makar', in which he elaborates the reasons for his attempt
to commit suicide in the town of Kazan in December 1887.
Over approximately the next twelve years his best work
consists almost exclusively of memoirs and reminiscences
in which he describes those spheres of Russian society
which he had known best during the closing decades of the
nineteenth century, brings before the reader portraits of
interesting people he had encountered during his varied
life, and sketches some aspects of the development of his
own personality up to the age of twenty-four, when he made
his debut as a writer. The best of these memoirs are marked
by a technical originality and reveal in the author powers
of observation and a profound psychological insight which
place them among the greatest in their genre in universal
literature.

The best known of Gorky's memoirs are his three autobiographical novels, *Childhood*, *My Apprenticeship*, and *My
Universities*. *Childhood* was written during the years 1912–
13, and it appeared in the newspaper *The Russian Word* in

K

instalments from 25 August 1913 to 30 January 1914; *My Apprenticeship* was written in 1914 and appeared fragmentarily in *The Russian Word* from 1 November to 6 December 1915; *My Universities*, written in 1922, was published in the magazine *Red Virgin Soil* from March to July 1923. Individual episodes in *My Universities* are illuminated in greater detail in 'An incident from the life of Makar' and in the sketch 'The Boss' written in 1912 and published in the issues of *The Contemporary* for March, April, and May 1913; this sketch is a full-length portrait of Vasili Semyonov, a master-baker of Kazan who was Gorky's principal employer in that city during his residence there between the ages of sixteen and twenty. The trilogy is based upon the author's experiences from 1871 to 1888, and Gorky continued the narrative in a series of fragmentary sketches beginning with 'The Watchman' and continuing with 'The Days of Korolenko', 'On the harm of philosophy', 'First Love', 'V. G. Korolenko'; these sketches were written in 1922–3 and deal with the years immediately prior to Gorky's debut as a writer. His original intention was to include *My Universities* with these sketches in a single volume to be entitled 'Among the intelligentsia'; he never realized this plan.

Childhood

The narrative of *Childhood* covers Alexei Peshkov's life from the age of three to eleven, beginning with the death of his father, Maxim Peshkov, at the age of 31 on 29 July 1871 in Astrakhan, and ending with the death of his mother, Varvara Peshkova, at the age of 37 on 5 August 1879 in Nizhny Novgorod. On his father's death Alexei and his mother return to her native town, Nizhny Novgorod, to live with her parents, Vasili and Akulina Kashirin, and he stays with them until, when his mother dies, Kashirin sends him out into the world to earn his own livelihood.

Vasili Kashirin was born about 1807 in the small town of Balakhna, the son of a soldier and a bun-seller. He worked for some time as a barge-hauler in the convoy of the Balakhna barge-owner, Baev, then took to textile dyeing, accumulated a certain amount of money, and opened his own dyeing establishment in Nizhny Novgorod. He prospered and was soon the owner of several establishments; on seven different occasions he was elected elder of the dyers' guild, and he represented his social class on the town council. His fortunes reached their peak in the mid-sixties, and in 1865 he built (as a status symbol) a fine wooden house in Kovalikha Street. By this time, however, the industrial expansion of Russia, greatly stimulated by the emancipation of the serfs and the Great Reforms of the early sixties, was gathering momentum and bringing commercial ruin to many untutored small businessmen like Kashirin. The second half of the sixties was a time of rapid decline for the Kashirin business, and in 1870 Vasili was obliged to sell his fine house and to move to a more modest residence on Uspensky Hill, where he and his family were living when Alexei and his mother joined them in the following year. The household consisted of the two old people, their sons, Mikhail and Yakov, Mikhail's wife, Natasha, and Alexey's two cousins, both called Sasha.

The eight childhood years which Alexei spends with the Kashirins bring about the break-up of their family and their complete impoverishment. First of all his Aunt Natasha dies in childbirth, then his uncles take their share of the family property and go to set up their own businesses on the other side of the river, then his mother remarries and quickly dies. In the meantime financial difficulties have obliged old Kashirin to move from house to house, attempting to ward off ruin by taking in lodgers, until finally he is reduced to living in two dark basement rooms in the slum quarter of Kunavino. Alexei's early childhood—of decisive importance in the formation of his personality—is spent

therefore against a family background of rapid impoverishment, constant removals, and never-ending squabbles
among his relatives, provoked by their misfortunes.
Childhood then is centred upon the story of the rapid
disintegration and impoverishment of a large lower-middle-
class Russian family, as seen through the eyes of a small boy
who watched it all happen. By virtue of this subject the
work possesses true epic and historical significance, because
joint families of the Kashirin type, and their kind of small
business, belonged to patriarchal Russia, the disintegration
of which was a fundamental part of Russian social history
in the second half of the nineteenth century. In *The Artomonov Business* Gorky showed the rise and fall of a large
capitalistic enterprise not, as we have seen, through analys-
ing economic processes but through the reactions of the
various members of the family; similarly in *Childhood* he is
interested predominantly in the behaviour of the three
generations of Kashirins in adversity. In his portrayal of
Vasili and Akulina he uses the well-tried literary device of
psychological contrast. We have already seen the different
kinds of Christianity professed by these two traditional
Russian types. Kashirin's philosophy of life faithfully reflects his religious beliefs; in its main features it strongly
resembles the outlook of the merchant priest Sylvester, the
author of the sixteenth-century manual of domestic behaviour *Domostroy*. In the mid-nineteenth-century, indeed,
the daily life and habits of thought of families of the urban
lower middle classes had changed little from the sixteenth.
Perhaps the most characteristically traditional attitude of
old Kashirin is his view of human beings as chattels who
serve him and may then be cast aside. One of his most
valuable employees, a youth nicknamed 'The Gypsy', is
killed through the masochistic stupidity of Yakov Kashirin;
the old man's reaction to this senseless destruction of an
attractive, talented young apprentice is to bemoan the fact
that in five years' time as a workman he would have been

worth his weight in gold. When he sends his grandson out into the world, Kashirin expounds his philosophy of life to him—bother only about yourself, because no one else will concern themselves about you, trust only yourself, achieve your ends through the exercise of strength and cunning. This outlook sits well upon the old man in the days of his prosperity, but recoils upon him in adversity; the ruin of his fortunes goes hand in hand with the destruction of his tyrannical paternal authority, and his children show no compassion for their defeated but still cantankerous and capricious patriarch. Kashirin himself degenerates into a feckless, complaining wretch—his last vestige of authority is destroyed when his daughter twice defies him over the choice of a husband. On the second occasion he can make no more effective protest than to retire in high dudgeon to the attic to read. Gorky presents a pathetic picture of this once masterful father and employer, with every shred of dignity stripped from him: 'He stood there, hanging on to the door-jamb, shrinking and going grey, as though dusted with ashes. Suddenly he went to the centre of the room, fell on his knees and slumped forward, supporting himself on his arm. Then he straightened up, beat himself on the breast with both hands and cried, "O God, O God".'

Akulina Kashirina is in every important respect the opposite of her husband. She is indifferent to both prosperity and adversity, because for her they both spring from the will of God and thus call for acceptance but not excessive elation or despair. Contrary to Kashirin, who is concerned only with the acquisition of wealth and power, she is preoccupied with human beings; thus she weeps for 'The Gypsy' because a fine young man, whom she loved, has been destroyed. Probably the most striking feature of her character, as opposed to her husband's, is that although he believes that God helps those who help themselves whereas she uncomplainingly accepts the dispensations of providence, in critical situations she is decisive and resourceful while Kashirin impotently wrings his hands. One incident in particular brings out the active element in her nature: a fire breaks out in the stables, and while her husband and the other members of the family yield to panic she leads out the horses and saves them. When she and Kashirin are living apart, after working all day she would often tramp almost five miles through the winter snow to see if he needed help. The manner of her death typifies both the Christian charity of her life and the benighted fecklessness of her family; one day in February 1887 while collecting alms for the poor, she slips and breaks her leg, develops gangrene, and dies because no one in the Kashirin household takes any action to save her.

Gorky's autobiographical trilogy and Tolstoy's, written sixty years before, are often compared and contrasted. A natural point of comparison between the first parts of each lies in the characters of Gorky's Akulina Ivanovna and Tolstoy's Natalya Savishna, the Irtenievs' housekeeper. In each work both of these personages are exceptional because in them the authors show religious feeling in an attractive light. In general Gorky depicts conventional religious devotion among the Russian lower classes as surviving only in degraded and unnatural forms; and among the upper classes Tolstoy shows it as the object of amused indifference. Typical of the superstition-ridden religious world of the lower classes in Gorky's work is the reaction of all the members of the Kashirin family except Akulina Ivanovna to the Gypsy's death; a characteristically upper-class ironical attitude to the Church in Tolstoy's world is that of Nicolai Irteniev's father.

Akulina and Natalya have much in common, because each possesses characteristics of outlook and personality which are based upon Orthodox piety. Natalya shares Akulina's conviction that acceptance of the ways of providence is an imperative Christian virtue—she accepts her imminent death with the same resignation as the other accepts her family's ruin and impoverishment. Both women, however, carry acceptance to a point where it ceases to be a virtue and becomes a vice because it makes them forget their dignity as individuals; at her master's command Natalya renounces her natural right to marriage and Akulina regards herself as her husband's possession, placed in his charge by God. In both Natalya and Akulina religious feeling is inextricably linked with serf mentality, but with piety and submissiveness both unite great practical ability as housekeepers. Natalya does not neglect her domestic duties even in her moment of inconsolable grief at the loss of her mistress, and Akulina makes the most she can of her family's depleted resources. Within the family circle both display great resourcefulness and initiative.

As their creators present them Akulina Ivanovna and Natalya Savishna show only one fundamental difference; Tolstoy wishes to present Natalya as a simple and sincere person contrasted sharply with the superficial, sophisticated representatives of the upper classes who surround her, and she appears therefore in a saintly light which mars her reality—Gorky, on the other hand, although he surrounds Akulina with the aura of the love he felt for her in childhood, has no ambition to depict her as a model of popular virtue, and he not only subjects to sharp criticism her religion of compassion and endurance but shows her as a prey to the vices of drink and snuff-taking. She appears as a delightfully real person, but she is no saint.

Alexei's father, Maxim Savvateich, as we have seen, dies when he is three, his mother, Varvara Vasilievna, eight years later. Necessarily therefore they both appear in the story of his childhood as fragmentary figures. His father is only a memory, a gay person who never beat him, played with him while he was ill with cholera, then suddenly vanished. He never enters the narrative except as recalled by other people, and everything they remember about him is good. In this way Gorky creates in his novel a dream of fatherhood which he never knew in reality. Because of his very early loss of his father he tends in later life to idealize paternal affection, and he takes pleasure in depicting warm relationships between father and son, like those between Ignat and Foma Gordeev or Saveli and Matvei Kozhemyakin.

Alexei's father is only an affectionately remembered shadow, but his mother possesses a concrete physical reality. 'She was clean, smooth and large, like a horse; she had a firm body and terribly strong hands.' Her son watches unhappily as grief and illness reduce this woman to a piteous slut; she repels his natural desire to establish an affectionate relationship with her because she bitterly resents the fact that he infected her husband with his fatal illness, and she thinks of him as a stone round her neck preventing her from escaping from her father's household, which she hates. Her harsh unrelenting nature makes her a true Kashirin, and her last action is to beat her son; she is however a tragic figure who twice in vain seeks in marriage the fulfilment of her cherished dream of the good life which might have made her a good person. A malevolent force seems to preside over the destinies of both of Alexei's parents. Again and again in Gorky's fictional world this same force destroys good people's dreams of happiness.

Tolstoy lost his mother at three, as Gorky lost his father. In his *Childhood* he presents Nikolai Irteniev's mother as the loving parent whom he never knew in real life, just as Gorky presents Maxim Peshkov as a tenderly preserved memory. Irtenieva appears before the reader in one short scene in which she has almost no physical reality; later we hear her voice in the letter she writes to her husband just before her death. Into her words of farewell in this letter Tolstoy puts all the tender affection which, had she lived, he might have expected to receive from his own mother: 'Farewell, dearest one, remember when I am no more that my love will never abandon you, wherever you may be.' Similarly, in the few memories which other characters relate of Alexei's father, Gorky conjures up all the companionship he might have enjoyed with this light-hearted, gentle man.

Gorky's memories of his two uncles were sporadic and devoid of affection. They tried once to drown his father in a hole in the ice because they resented the fact that he had a claim to some part of the family property. Alexei's irregular and infrequent meetings with his uncles and cousins after they have all left their father's home shows how completely the bonds of the once united Kashirin family were severed once their commercial prosperity was destroyed. The only positive quality revealed by all these close relatives is a gift for music shared by Uncle Yakov and his son, Sasha. In Gorky's work we last hear of Sasha Yakovich as a chorister in a famous Nizhny Novgorod church choir.

Outside the Kashirin family circle in childhood Alexei Peshkov enjoys a short friendship with the three small sons of a neighbour, Colonel Ovsyannikov. The fact that such a family could find themselves the neighbours of petty merchants like the Kashirins demonstrates the mixing up of classes which took place during these decades of social upheaval in Russia. In his description of Alexei's relations with these boys, Gorky shows how the natural attraction of children for one another is overcome by class barriers erected by their elders. Accustomed to the malevolent squabbling which went on among all the members of the Kashirin family, Alexei is most struck among the Ovsyannikov boys by their concern for each other; if the youngest falls down, the other two 'laughed as people always laugh at someone who falls down, but there was nothing spiteful in their laughter; they would immediately help him to get up and if he had dirtied his hands or knees they wiped them with burdock leaves or their handkerchiefs'. These words betray Gorky's sense of loss of the affectionate family life he never knew in childhood.

Throughout his trilogy Gorky shows a marked weakness for portraying eccentrics. The reason for this was probably that he was always attracted by the unusual in whatever form he found it in life and among people; the great men whose acquaintance he made when he was famous stood out from the average run through their exceptional abilities, but among ordinary men and women he was tempted to look for the unusual in oddities of physical appearance or quirks of personality. In childhood he knew only ordinary people. The strangest character in *Childhood* is the repulsive old drayman, Uncle Pyotr; Gorky writes of him, 'I found it more and more impossible to look upon him as anything but a boy like myself, dressed up as an old man.' Pyotr is disgusting in his triviality, so inappropriate to his grey hairs; he pursues a personal vendetta against his nine-year-old erstwhile friend. As relics of Russia's evil past, old men in Gorky's trilogy usually threaten the victory of good over evil in the development of Alexei's personality. It finally emerges that with two accomplices Pyotr has been living through robbing churches; he cuts his throat when the police discover his crimes. Alexei then realises that like Kashirin he was a pathetic, not a fearsome figure.

My Apprenticeship

The narrative of this second part of the trilogy covers the years from the end of 1879, when Alexei takes his first employment as an odd-job boy in Leonti Porkhunov's shoe shop in Nizhny Novgorod, to June 1884, when he leaves his home town for Kazan. Although the time span of this work is therefore only five years as compared with the eight of *Childhood*, it is two-thirds as long again; this is partly because a man's memories of his years from eleven to sixteen are naturally more numerous than those of his earliest childhood, but also because *My Apprenticeship* suffers from prolixity as opposed to the dramatic tautness of the narrative of *Childhood*. It lacks the cohesive interest which is provided in the earlier volume by the story of the impoverishment and moral degeneration of the Kashirins. It contains no similar central theme. The focal point of Alexei's life during his years of adolescence is the household of his grandmother's sister, Matryona Sergeeva, where he spends three separate spells, from the autumn of 1880 to the spring of 1881, from the autumn of 1881 to the spring of 1882, and from the spring of 1883 to the autumn of 1884. He tells us all that is typical about this household in his account of the first spell; much in his description of the second and third is therefore superfluous.

The Sergeev household consists of Matryona Sergeeva, her elder son Valentin and his wife, and her younger son Viktor. The whole family enjoys moderate prosperity from Valentin's business as a draughtsman and building contractor; Alexei joins them originally as apprentice to Valentin, but Matryona fears that his presence might prejudice the future of her younger son, whom she loves obsessively, and she burdens him with domestic duties to prevent him learning the business. The chief characteristics of the household are self-righteousness, hatred and distrust of every evidence in other people of noble qualities they themselves lack, well-fed indolence, adulation of money, contempt for the weak, and fawning admiration for the strong; these were all widespread vices in commercial Russian society during the early eighteen-eighties, and Gorky presents the Sergeev way of life as a concrete symbol of a social atmosphere. To Alexei, as to many radical Russian thinkers of the time, it seems that this way of life will last for ever. His reaction is an hysterical urge to crawl into a corner and 'howl like a dog'. There seemed little else anyone could do at that time. In their works the poet Nadson and the short story writer Garshin were in their own way 'howling like dogs'.

Alexei's years with the Kashirins and later with the Sergeevs are his only experience in childhood of family life;

the only evidence he sees in both families of normal affection among kinsmen is the mutual love of his grandparents, which survives, even though sorely tried, in old age and adversity. Matryona Sergeeva's love for her younger son is morbidly possessive, and he repays it with contempt. There are no characters in *My Apprenticeship* who compare in epic significance with Vasili and Akulina Kashirin, none who like these two in *Childhood* are present throughout the narrative. Whereas the action in *Childhood* remains within the Kashirin family, in *My Apprenticeship* it moves freely in the wake of Alexei's various jobs. In addition to his three periods of service with the Sergeevs, he spends some time in a shoe shop, makes two trips on Volga river-steamers, works in an icon-painting workshop, and acts as overseer for Valentin Sergeev at a fair-ground which the latter is constructing. This mobile life means that he knows no one for very long, and the characters who come before the reader are therefore episodic, inter-related only because they are all acquaintances of Alexei.

One of the most significant characters in this volume is the fashionable widow who lives for a while in the flat below the Sergeevs and to whom Alexei gives the name Queen Margot because she represents for him a dream of regal beauty in the middle of a way of life compounded of his relatives' baseness of soul and the near-animal behaviour of the soldiers and washerwomen who work near by. In reality this woman is the mistress of one of the officers but her youthful admirer cannot believe that so much beauty can be associated with the kind of love-making he sees among the soldiers and washerwomen. In his portrayal of Queen Margot Gorky re-creates not the real person but the dream of perfect beauty Alexei sees in her. He tells us: 'I embellished my memories of Queen Margot with all the beauty I had culled from books; I bestowed upon her the finest of what lay within me—all the loveliest fantasies born of my reading.' Alexei's youthful vision of this quite ordinary woman is the kind of delightful illusion without which in those harsh years he could not have lived. Gorky surrounds her in his story with the scent of flowers, the sound of music, and the charm and majesty of poetry. In the end, however, reality breaks in upon Alexei's dream—he finds her one day in her lover's arms. The blow to his cherished illusion is not softened by the fact that this man is a lover of poetry and music. 'I felt that I had lost something and for several days I was profoundly grieved.'

One of the most sympathetic characters in *My Apprenticeship* is the washerwoman Natalya Kozlovskaya. As Gorky presents her, her most attractive characteristic is the same active capacity to deal with the hardships of life as that which he admired in his grandmother. All the other washerwomen harm their hands through hard scrubbing, but Kozlovskaya has the good sense to make and wear a pair of leather gauntlets. She makes great sacrifices to secure a good education for her daughter, but the latter, having become a governess, abandons her. She dies of tuberculosis after spending her last years as a prostitute. Gorky tells of her fate with profound compassion, because, although the misfortunes of feckless people did not unduly distress him, he was deeply moved when, as often happened, he saw active and resourceful people through no fault of their own overtaken by disaster.

From November 1882 to April 1883, Alexei Peshkov works in an icon-painting establishment owned by a drunken widow, I. Ya. Salabanova. Typically, Gorky's description of these months in *My Apprenticeship* deals predominantly with the personalities of Alexei's fellow workmen. The conditions of work in the establishment are bestial. Against this background Alexei looks among his colleagues for any signs of talent or nobility of spirit. The Cossack Kapendyukhin is a magnificent singer, the fifteen-year-old Pavel Odintsov a gifted sketcher, Zhikarev a craftsman of incomparable skill; the convinced atheist Sitanov provides for his mistress even though she has infected him with venereal disease and between him and Kapendyukhin there exists a bond of unbreakable friendship (an infrequent relationship in Gorky's world). The youth Davydov, dying of consumption, faces his fate with humorous courage.

Among these men, however, the best in human nature exists side by side with the worst. Kapendyukhin was a drunkard, Zhikarev indulges in sexual orgies with his repulsive mistress, and the old man Gogolev is filthy in his personal habits and treacherous in his relations with his fellow workers.

Zhikarev's mistress is one of those disgusting oddities who abound in Gorky's work and who seems to him to be an offence to the dignity of mankind: 'Six and a half feet tall, although she was over forty her round expressionless face with its enormous horsy eyes was still fresh and smooth and her tiny mouth seemed painted on, like that of a cheap doll.'

In all there are twenty icon painters. They are one of many groups of Russian people in Gorky's work through whose corporate psychology he tries to suggest traits of national character. Another such group is formed by the passengers on the river-steamer *Dobry*. Certain reflections, inspired in him by the passengers, are renewed among the painters. Of the passengers he writes:

The most striking thing about people is their shyness and timidity and melancholy resignation and it is strange and terrible when this crust of resignation is suddenly broken through in moments of brutal merrymaking that are rarely entertaining.

[of the painters] Merriment is never long-lived among us and is not valued for its own sake but evoked with great effort as an antidote to the brooding Russian heartache. There is nothing durable about a merriment which has no independent existence nor any will to survive but comes only to brighten dreary days.

Only too often Russian merriment turns unexpectedly and imperceptibly into cruel drama. In the middle of a dance, in which the dancer seems to be unravelling himself of his bonds, the animal in him will suddenly break loose and with bestial frenzy throw itself at everyone and everything, roaring, raging, shattering. . . .

Of the passengers again: 'I felt that people did not know where they were being taken and it made no difference to them where the steamer put them off: wherever they landed, they would remain ashore for only a short time before boarding this or some other steamer which would again take them somewhere; all of them were homeless wanderers, all lands were alien to them and they were all complete cowards'; and of the painters: 'All their talk, while giving me some insight into life, revealed it as a kind of dreary vacuum in which people, like dry leaves on the surface of a windswept pond, drift about without aim or purpose, themselves resenting and denouncing the aimlessness of their drifting.' Among groups of Russians Gorky notices usually only negative qualities, some traditional, like the tendency to outbursts of unbridled debauchery, others, like purposelessness and bewilderment, fostered by the disintegration of old Russian society in the late nineteenth century. In individuals he is always looking for the corresponding virtues to set against group defects—strength to resist the influence of one's surroundings, humanity, temperamental stability, decisiveness.

Nothing perhaps can better illustrate the animal-like character of much lower-class Russian merriment in Tsarist days than Gorky's brilliant and horrible description of Zhikarev's dance with his enormous mistress:

Zhikarev did not know how to dance. He simply shifted his feet, tapping with the heels of his shiny boots or taking little goat-leaps, out of time with the music. His feet seemed not to belong to him, and he twisted his body in a horrible manner, like a wasp in a web or a fish in a net. It was a sad spectacle. . . . She too was a poor dancer. She could only swing her huge body slowly and shift it noiselessly from place to place. In her left hand she held a handkerchief which she waved languidly; she kept her right hand on her hip and this gave her the look of an enormous jug.

Conflicting emotions flitted across Zhikarev's face as he kept circling about this statue. It seemed that not he alone was dancing there but ten men, all different: one was shy and modest, another crabbed and intimidating; a third was himself intimidated and gave little cries as he tried to slip away from that colossal repellent woman. Suddenly another appeared baring his teeth and twisting his body like a wounded dog. This ugly dance oppressed me and roused evil memories of soldiers and cooks and laundresses and dogmating.

The repulsive impression of this dance is intensified by the background: 'The faceless icons stared down from the dark walls, the dark night pressed against the window-panes, the lamps burned low in the stuffy workshop. Above the stamping of feet and the hum of voices, I could catch the sound of water dripping quickly from the copper wash-basin into the slop bucket.' Animal-like behaviour in human beings worries Sitanov and is one of the causes of his atheism, for if there is a God, and He made people in His image, how can they fall so short of His perfection? Alexei finds no answer to this. It is, as we have seen, one of the roots of Matvei's atheism in *Confession*.

My Universities

The narrative of this, the third volume of the trilogy, covers the years from June 1884 to September 1888 and takes Alexei from the ages of sixteen to twenty. Unlike the earlier volumes *My Universities* is undivided into chapters, but the narrative falls naturally into two parts, the first set in Kazan and ending with Alexei's attempted suicide in December 1887; the second set in the village of Krasno-vidovo, thirty miles down the Volga from Kazan, and cover-ing only the three months from June to September 1888. Despite its much greater time span the first part is only half as long again as the second; the reason for this is that in his customary style Gorky describes his three-year sojourn in Kazan through presenting interesting people he knew there, while his three months in the country are related as a sustained narrative, the theme of which is the struggle of the Populist, Mikhail Romas' little group of radicals (of whom Alexei is one) to persuade the small peasant fruit-growers of the area to organize collectives in order to keep themselves independent of the large buyers. With this central subject is linked Gorky's description of how, under the wise and realistic teaching of Romas, Alexei gradually regains his mental balance and self-confidence after his unsuccessful attempt at suicide. Constructed around these two closely linked themes, the second part of *My Universities* emerges in its own right as one of the best of Gorky's long stories.

The years from sixteen to twenty in a young man's life are a period when he is particularly susceptible to the influence of new ideas. The significance of the title *My Universities* lies in the fact that although Alexei Peshkov's original intention in going to Kazan was to enter the university, he was unsuccessful, and during the next four years he becomes acquainted with a bewildering variety of ideas not principally from books but from people. Gorky writes in *My Universities*: 'I seldom found ideas in books which I had not already encountered in real life.' The principal interest of this book lies in the impact upon the untutored youth of the diverse, often contradictory, views which he hears from people of all kinds with whom he comes into contact; as he approaches manhood he strives to discover which opinions suit him best and to which category of people he belongs. The drama of his life during these years (which nearly ends in tragedy) lies in his inner struggles to find himself. He fails.

Gorky's art in *My Universities*—the linking of a man's opinions with the whole man—is Dostoevskian. In various novels written during the years 1906–12—*The Life of Matvei Kozhemyakin* and *Mother* for example—he had attempted to base characterization upon ideology, but had succeeded only in making his characters vehicles for the expression of political opinions, without giving them any reality as people. He does not repeat this failure in *My*

Universities. Each character in this book is alive and memorable.

The revolutionary movement in Russia of the eighteen-eighties is represented in *My Universities* by the Populist Mikhail Romas and the saintly figure of Andrei Derenkov, the baker who sees his function in life as financial provider for impoverished radical intellectuals, whom he considers the salt of the earth. Romas is the son of a blacksmith of Chernigov, and being thus of humble birth knows the Russian people in their vices as well as their virtues and is not tempted, like well-born revolutionaries, to idealize them. In this he is at one with Alexei. The peasant, he thinks, should be told: 'You're not a bad fellow, as far as that goes; but the life you live is bad, and you don't know how to do the smallest thing to make it easier and better.' He understands perfectly the peasants' attitude to the conditions of their emancipation: 'The peasant is a Tsarist. Many masters, he feels, are a bad thing; one master, not so bad. He is waiting for a day when the Tsar will explain to him the real significance of freedom. And then, let everyone grab what he can.' Unlike many Russian thinkers who knew nothing of the realities of the Russian people, Romas does not delude himself that a revolution can be engineered overnight:

> Make the peasant understand that he must learn little by little to take the Tsar's power into his own hands; explain to him that the people must have the right to elect their officials from their own ranks —to elect their police officer, their governor, and the Tsar, also. . . .
> 'But that will take a hundred years.'
> 'Did you expect to do it by Trinity Sunday?'

Romas's physical characteristics reflect the realism and balance of his political views. We read of the 'quiet contemplation' of his grey eyes, his 'powerfully-moulded frame', his reserve. Nothing upsets him. 'It somehow seemed to me that where this man's soul should have been he had

some kind of mechanism wound up like clockwork to run
evenly all his life.'

Andrei Derenkov's devotion to the revolutionary cause
matches his father's religious devotion. Gentleness is the
distinguishing characteristic of both. Apart from Andrei
there are two younger brothers, Alexei and Ivan, and a
sister Maria who later marries Romas. This is the only
family in Gorky's trilogy whom he shows as united by love.
Alexei Peshkov imagines himself in love with Maria. In
marrying Romas this girl prepares for herself a life of self-
sacrifice, because of the next fifteen years he spent ten in
Siberian exile. He died in 1920.

In *My Universities*, in his depiction of the Tolstoyan
Klopsky and the meek-mannered tailor Mednikov, Gorky
continues his long-standing polemic with the moral teaching
of Tolstoy and Dostoevsky. Klopsky is one of the most
repellent characters in the trilogy. The author describes
him as 'one of those men—of frenzied faith in the salvation
of the world by the power of love—who are prepared in
pure compassion to rend and burn their fellow humans'.
His appearance is repugnant—raw-boned, thick negroid
lips, hairy hands. Living with two sisters he attempts to
seduce them both on the same day. Mednikov's meekness
conceals a streak of sadistic cruelty: '. . . he regularly
thrashed his children, a girl of seven and a boy of eleven,
with a triple-thonged leather whip and beat his wife across
the calves of the legs with a bamboo stick.'

Every manifestation of religious belief in the characters
of *My Universities* is in some way repulsive or absurd. Even
Andrei Derenkov's gentle father develops religious melan-
cholia. In a lodging-house where Alexei lives for some time
he meets a student who is determined to prove the existence
of God by higher mathematics but dies before he succeeds.
Virulent atheism, on the other hand, Gorky presents in the
attractive character Yakov Shaposhnikov, a fitter dying of
tuberculosis. In Dostoevskian manner this man seems to be

devoting every moment of life remaining to him to the demolition of God. Having read the Bible he decided that all the Church's teaching was made up and the intensity of his resultant disbelief matches the absoluteness of his earlier faith. He dies and Gorky writes of him: '. . . here a man lived on this earth—Yakov a lone soul fighting God with all the power of his spirit; and he has died an ordinary death. Perfectly ordinary. There was something very slighting about that, something very hard to bear.' In Gorky's view a Dostoevskian atheist like Shaposhnikov should have had a Dostoevskian death, like Kirillov's.

Ideas and philosophies appear in *My Universities* as living things, each of them challenging the troubled youth who stands at the centre of the narrative to discover the truth about them and to decide which of them best answers his personal uncertainties. In this work, as in the other two parts of the trilogy, we receive little direct information about the inner life of Alexei Peshkov, but we are more strongly aware of his presence. We sense throughout that an intense spiritual ferment is going on within him which taxes every ounce of his physical and emotional strength. His attempted suicide brings a momentary relief from the growing tension of the preceding narrative. This incident is followed by a short period of repose and recuperation in the countryside, but the inner conflicts which provoked it soon renew themselves and the last three years of Peshkov's life, before he takes on the identity of M. Gorky the writer, are marked by repeated temptations to destroy himself. Much of the emotional force of Gorky's early stories springs from his spiritual unrest during these years. The act of creative writing calms this unrest and at the same time answers one of the writer's most persistent questions of himself—what kind of person am I and what is my task in life? Gorky tells us of the wonder which he felt when he discovered his talent—'to be a writer—I had never dreamed of that'; when in September 1892 he sat down in Tiflis and wrote 'Makar Chudra' he brought to a happy ending the tortured youthful pilgrimage of the orphan from Nizhny Novgorod which five years before had almost ended in tragedy.

Style of the narrative

Gorky's narrative technique in his trilogy is distinctive and constitutes a considerable part of the originality of the work. This technique is clearly illustrated in Chapters 1 and 4 of *Childhood*.

The events described in Chapter 1 of *Childhood* occupied in real life probably about six weeks, from the end of July to the middle of September 1871. The central incident of these weeks was the journey up the Volga by river-steamer from Astrakhan to Nizhny Novgorod made by Alexei Peshkov with his mother and grandmother after the death of his father. Gorky gives us only the vaguest indication of how long this journey lasted: 'Steamboats moved slowly forty years ago. It took us a long time to reach Nizhny Novgorod. . . .' Of the many days the voyage lasted he picks out two which are marked by a special incident and reproduces them through a scenic evocation of this incident. On the first of these two days the steamer arrives at Saratov and his baby brother, Maxim, who had died soon after the beginning of the journey, is carried ashore and buried; on the second the voyage ends at Nizhny Novgorod, the travellers are met by the rest of the Kashirin family, and they all walk together up the hill to their house.

The day at Saratov is recounted in five scenes. In the first we see Alexei with his mother and grandmother waiting in their cabin for the boat to dock; the baby's body lies on a table in the corner, wrapped in white cloth, and its mother leans against the wall, her hands behind her head, her eyes tightly closed in grief. The whole vessel shakes from the vibration of the engines.

The second scene shows the arrival at Saratov; a broad-shouldered, grey-haired sailor brings a small box into the cabin, the baby's body is placed in it, and the two women carry it out. On the way grandmother has to turn sideways to pass through the cabin door. The third scene is enacted between Alexei and the sailor, who remains behind in the cabin after the women have gone. Their conversation is a model of a conversation between a little boy and a man he has never seen before:

'Who are you?'
'A sailor.'
'And who's Saratov?'
'A city. Look out of the window. There it is.'
.   .   .   .   .   .
'Where did grandmother go?'
'To bury her grandson.'
'Will they put him in the ground?'
'Of course they will.'

The fourth scene shows Alexei alone in the cabin after the boat has docked and the sailor has gone to assist passengers to land. He comes out into the passage and, looking up, catches sight of people with bags and bundles in their hands leaving the boat; with childish logic he decides he too must leave and he goes on deck. The passengers shout at him, buffet him, and ask him who he is. The sailor reappears and takes him back to the cabin.

In the fifth scene Alexei is alone in the cabin, the boat motionless, everything quiet. Panic-striken, he imagines he has been left alone for ever. He hurls a bottle of milk at the door knob. The bottle breaks and the milk floods his shoes. He lies down and cries himself to sleep. So ends the day.

Two details from these scenes—his grandmother passing sideways through the door and the broken milk-bottle—illustrate the essentially visual nature of Gorky's memory. As a boy he seems to have noticed everything and as a man to have forgotten nothing he saw.

The day of the arrival at Nizhny is announced without preamble: 'I remember my grandmother's childlike joy on catching sight of Nizhny.' We see the city through the old woman's eyes: 'Look at the domes of the churches—as if they were flying.' Gorky wastes no more words upon the city, but keeps the action moving: 'A large boat filled with people approached our steamer and hooked on to the lowered gangplank up which the people climbed on to our deck. At the head of them rushed a small lean old man in a long black coat. He had green eyes, a hooked nose and a beard red as gold.' The family reunion which follows is described almost entirely in dialogue. In a few expressive lines Gorky sketches the little group, and they then proceed all together up the hill to their fine house: 'It was painted a dirty pink and had bulging windows with the roof pulled down low over them.'

The scenic description of the two most eventful days of the voyage from Astrakhan to Nizhny Novgorod forms the greater part but not the whole of Gorky's account of it; these two days are linked in the narrative by a striking picture of grandmother as she appeared on the journey to her three-year-old grandson. This picture flows out of the narrative, beginning on the first day after she has asked Alexei why he broke the milk-bottle; and rejoins it on the second day after Gorky has described how much she liked telling folk-tales to passengers and crew. Akulina's ecstatic remark to her grandson that the domes of the churches of Nizhny Novgorod look as if they were flying harmonizes with the imagery of the folk-tales she has told throughout the journey about 'saints, animals, chivalrous bandits and dark forces'. Around the figure of his beloved grandmother Gorky constructs a generalized picture of the voyage as it proceeds on days marked by no particular incident: 'At supper they would treat her to vodka and me to watermelon and cantaloupe; this was all done on the sly because there was a man on board who forbade the eating of fruit.

If he caught anyone with fruit he would grab it away and toss it into the river. He was dressed like a guard with brass buttons down his uniform, and was always drunk.' Incident and character, character and incident, this is the essential style of Gorky's narrative.

Alexei Peshkov's journey up the Volga to Nizhny Novgorod probably took about three weeks; with his mother and grandmother, after his father's death, he probably spent a similar period of time in Astrakhan before setting out for Nizhny. Gorky describes these weeks in a manner similar to his description of his voyage—by picking out two days marked by special events. Few authors can have begun an autobiographical novel with a more dramatic scene. The three-year-old boy, concealed behind a trunk, watches in terror while his mother in agony gives birth to his brother; in her struggles she repeatedly bumps her husband's corpse lying in the corner beneath the window. From this stark scene of the beginning of a human life Gorky moves on without pause or stylistic modulation to the occasion of Alexei's father's funeral; typically, he limits himself to the moment of the burial, unconcerned with auxiliary events. He describes a rainy day and frogs trying to jump out of the newly dug grave but being beaten back by lumps of clay. From Alexei's stream of consciousness he picks out his surprise when his grandmother asks him why he does not cry; 'I was not easily moved to tears', writes the author.

The opening scene of *Childhood* is invented; we know from parish records that Maxim Peshkov was buried on 30 July 1871, and his second son born on 1 August. The essential truth of the scene, however, lies in the manner in which, through the juxtaposition of birth and death, it communicates the fearful suffering of Alexei's mother during these few days. She is absent from the funeral: 'The only people at the grave were the dripping guard on duty, two grumpy peasants with spades, my grandmother and I.' On the steamer she is overwhelmed by grief of an intensity which the reader can only imagine, since to the very recent loss of her husband has been added that of her new-born son. With Varvara Peshkova at their centre these early pages set the tone of the entire subsequent narrative, in which the most tragic catastrophes seem to form part of the normal course of an individual's life. Involuntarily one recalls the contrast of the petty misfortune which overtakes Nikolai Irteniev at the beginning of Tolstoy's trilogy—his tutor swats a fly above his bed and he is awakened by the dead creature falling upon his head.

Chapter 1 of *Childhood* recounts about six weeks of Gorky's earliest childhood. Chapter 4 deals with the whole of the winter of 1871-2. It is placed in time by the fact that we are told that an important incident in Chapter 3 occurs at the beginning of winter, and Chapter 5 begins: 'The division of property was made that spring. . . .' The narrative consists of a judicious mixture of the general and the particular which is typical of the narrative of the trilogy as a whole. From the entire winter Gorky picks out two nights, the first of which is noteworthy because it is described through the medium of one of the very few happy scenes contained in the book—Alexei and his grandmother are in bed together, grandmother pulls the edge of the quilt and he flies into the air. The second night is one of the most eventful he spends with the Kashirins—the workshops are burnt down, the excitement of this incident makes Aunt Natalya give premature birth, and she dies. Just as in Chapter 1 the two particularized days of the river voyage are linked by a description of grandmother's personality as it was revealed during the voyage, so the two nights described in Chapter 4 are linked by Gorky's depiction of her religious life. Again, as in Chapter 1, this general picture joins up naturally with the particular occurrences on each side of it; grandmother prays for a long time on the first night before getting into bed, and this gives Gorky the opportunity to record a long prayer typical of those she habitually says after days of quarrels and fighting among her family. This prayer conveys admirably her attitude to God as a kind, understanding father to whom one may speak as one speaks to human beings one loves. From his general picture of Akulina's religious life, Gorky passes easily to the night of the fire because she is on her knees when her husband dashes into the bedroom to raise the alarm. From this point on the narrative proceeds without interruption to the end of the events of that fateful night. Gorky's account of the catastrophes of this night is one of the best pieces of consecutive narrative in his trilogy. He was irresistibly attracted by fires—as by all elemental forces—and few writers have described them more vividly.

The snow gleamed red with the flames and the walls of the outhouses swayed and trembled as though straining towards the corner of the yard where the fire was burning merrily, lighting up the broad cracks in the workshop and thrusting its bright, twisted tongues through them. Red and gold ribbons of flame slid quickly over the dry boards of the roof where the slender clay chimney, thrusting dynamically upwards, poured a thin stream of smoke into the air. A soft crackling and silken rustling beat at the windowpane; the fire grew, and its splendour transformed the workshop into beauty like that of the iconostasis in the church, luring the watcher with irresistible force.

Rarely also can a writer have described more dramatically the scene in a household when a woman gives birth to a child and dies in so doing. Gorky recounts this incident through depicting the commotion which it provokes among the family. 'Once more everything became topsy-turvy in the house, as during the fire.' Gorky is at his best in evoking a scene made up of constant movement, dramatic tension, and spasmodic conversation. Natalya's ceaseless agonized wails fill the house; doors slam, people run about, Alexei gets in his Uncle Mikhail's way, and Mikhail picks him up and beats him against the stove so that he becomes unconscious. He is still unconscious when his aunt dies. When he comes

to he sees evidence of what has been going on in the presence
of a priest and a military doctor. His Uncle Yakov takes him
to bed and tells him of his aunt's death. The events of this
single night have forced upon his attention all the ignorance, backwardness, and brutality of his family. These
are summed up in a shout he had heard before he fell foul
of his uncle: 'Give her some lamp oil with rum and soot in
it: half a glass of oil, half a glass of rum and a tablespoon of
soot. . . .' As he lies in bed, when all is over, he suffers one
of his darkest moments of childish despair: 'My head, or
perhaps my heart, seemed to swell up; everything I had
seen in that house dragged through me like a sledge along a
wintry road, pressing me down, annihilating me. . . .' Before
he goes to sleep his grandmother enters the room, complaining of the agonizing pain of her hands, which she had burnt
while putting out the fire.

This chapter, which takes in a whole winter, ends as it
begins with Alexei Peshkov in bed waiting for his grandmother to join him. Ironically, the disastrous events which
make up the chapter and the way of life of the Kashirin
household described in it directly contradict the old woman's
faith, which she expresses in her prayers—that God has
created on earth a splendid life for people. This contradiction is clearly illustrated in the contrast between the happiness of the opening scene of the chapter and the mood of
sadness on which it ends. In the next chapter, however,
Akulina Ivanovna's first words show the indestructible resilience of her faith: 'Praised be the saints and angels to the
end of time! At last, Alyosha my pigeon, we've come to a
quiet life.' Alyosha is not so sure: 'But I did not find our
life very quiet.'

The narrative technique of Gorky's trilogy may be described as dramatic impressionism. The predominant characteristics of life, as he recreates it, are constant action
and movement, lively conversation, frequent meetings and
partings, ever-changing impressions. The narrative flows

on, uninterrupted by lengthy descriptions of people or places, reproducing the stream of life, re-creating its texture. The personalities of Alexei Peshkov, the poor boy, or the reflections of Maxim Gorky, the eminent writer, rarely intrude between the world of the book and the reader; yet, having read it, we know fairly well what kind of person the central character is. He reveals himself to us as the years pass, becoming a more and more substantial figure as he grows up. This is natural.

In his trilogy Gorky presents Alexei Peshkov as a boy and youth without a single imperfection of character. By doing so he makes Alexei's many enemies seem wickeder and his few friends nobler, and underlines the evil nature of a society in which such a person is constantly threatened with annihilation.

Alexei Peshkov is the only character who remains before the eyes of the reader thoughout Gorky's trilogy. Other people come and go as he meets with them. Only his grandparents are present in the narrative for a prolonged period of time, and even they appear only sporadically after 1879 when *Childhood* ends. The last mention of them both belongs to the year 1887 when they die within a short time of each other. His father, as we have seen, is dead before the narrative opens, and his mother in *Childhood* is present only intermittently; she will not stay among the Kashirins. Other characters who play important parts in his childhood and youth are present usually only for a few months; he knows Smury from May to October 1881, Pavel Odintsov from January to April 1883, and Mikhail Romas from June to August 1888. Generally speaking the space which the characters occupy in the story corresponds to the length of time Alexei knows them; the most noteworthy exception to this rule is the French teacher of history, Georges (in *My Universities*), whom he meets only on one occasion. Gorky relates this encounter at length because of the violent impact which Georges's ideas make upon the nineteen-year-old

Peshkov. By far the greater number of Alexei's acquaintances are, indeed, like Georges, friends of an hour; and Gorky disposes of them in a few lines drawing attention to a physical peculiarity, an eccentricity of character, or an outlandish opinion. Typical examples of this kind of fleeting appearance are: in *Childhood* the one-eyed beggar, Nikitushka, 'a bearded old man with a red coal in the place of his right eye, and his left tightly shut'; in *My Universities*, the veterinary surgeon, Lavrov, 'yellow and swollen with dropsy, panting for breath', who thinks that 'cruelty should be increased until people get sick of it everywhere' and commits suicide with potassium cyanide rather than wait for the dropsy to kill him. Gorky has a twofold reason for introducing so many of these lightning sketches into his narrative; the first is that they allow him to indulge his eye for physical or psychological eccentricity, and the second that they communicate to the reader the impression of a way of life in which the accidental and transitory nature of personal relationships reflects the chaotic social background. In the world of Tolstoy's autobiographical trilogy people meet, part, and meet again through the force of social custom; Irteniev, for example, re-meets Sonya Valakhina, a childhood friend, after three years' interval because, after spending some time in Moscow, he is required by convention to call upon her family before leaving again for the country. In Gorky's world, by contrast, people meet and part by pure chance and once having parted rarely meet again; in *My Universities*, for example, Peshkov meets the weaver Nikolai Rubtsov through taking his side in a fight in a public house, and after a short but warm friendship parts with him again when, both having been arrested in a scuffle outside a brothel, he breaks away from the police, leaving Rubtsov in custody. In Tolstoy's world accident (death, for example) might prevent re-meetings; in Gorky's it is the only factor which brings them about.

2

Apart from his autobiographical trilogy, Gorky's best known reminiscences are contained in his memoirs of famous people he had known, and in certain of the short sketches in his two collections *Through Russia* (1912–17) and *Notes from my Diary* (1922–3). Of the first the greatest is his 'Memories of Tolstoy', written in 1918–19 and based upon the acquaintance of the two writers in the Crimea in the winter and spring of 1901–2.

At the turn of the century contemporary Russian literature was summed up for Western readers in the names of Tolstoy, Chekhov, and Gorky. In the early months of 1901 the health of the three men was extremely bad and by a fortunate chance they all, on medical advice, took up residence the following winter in the Crimea. Tolstoy lived from September to June 1902 on the estate of his friend Countess Panina at Gaspra, Gorky from November to April at Oleiz, and Chekhov from October to May at Anura near Yalta. With Gorky lived Leopold Antonovich Suler-zhitsky, the talented, anarchically minded son of a Kiev book-binder. In the course of a short life (1872–1916) this man worked as a painter, a Tolstoyan propagandist, a deep-sea sailor and a producer with the Arts Theatre. He helped to organize the emigration of the Caucasian dukhobory to Canada. All who knew him loved him for his gentle, expansive nature.

During this winter the four men had frequent meetings. Gorky's memoir is based upon the copious notes he made after each encounter. In November 1906, when he left Russia for seven years, he gave his notes into his wife's keeping. On 3 November 1910, while living on Capri, Gorky heard of Tolstoy's flight from his home and under the impact of this event he began a letter to his old friend and literary mentor, Korolenko. On the night of 3/4 November false rumours arose about Tolstoy's death and on the

4th reports based upon these rumours appeared in London, Paris, and Rome newspapers; on the 4th Gorky received a telegram from Russia communicating the false news and he continued his unfinished letter to Korolenko with the words 'Lev Tolstoy is dead'. In the evening he wrote to the critic Amfiteatrov and closed his letter with the remark that he had just heard that the rumour of Tolstoy's death was unfounded. Tolstoy died on the 7th.

The finished version of Gorky's sketch consists of the notes he had made in the Crimea together with his letter to Korolenko which he never completed and never sent. He tells us that he made no changes in the text of the letter. *Memories of Tolstoy* is not an essay written by one writer about another, but the story of a short period of friendship between two very percipient men. It is essentially a dramatic fragment in which the centre of the stage is occupied by Tolstoy and his young chronicler and the minor characters are Chekhov and Sulerzhitsky. The dramatic quality of the writing springs from the tension which underlay the relationship between the two men. Gorky tells us that at his first meeting with Tolstoy (on 13 January 1900 at Tolstoy's Moscow house) he felt that he was being subjected to an examination by a nobleman who spoke to him condescendingly in a 'popular style'; and in another place he remarks that Tolstoy's interest in him was primarily ethnographical, 'I am in his eyes an individual from a tribe little known to him.' We have already seen (page 38) Gorky's hostility to Tolstoyan moral teaching. Tolstoy, for his part, told Chekhov: 'I cannot be frank with Gorky, I do not know why, but I cannot. . . . Gorky is a spiteful person. He is like a seminarist who was forced to take the cowl and then became embittered at everything. He has the soul of a peeping Tom, he has come from somewhere to a land of Canaan which is alien to him and he peers at everything, observes everything and bears a report about it all to some God of his own.' Tolstoy was well aware of Gorky's antipathy to his moralizing and he never expounded his favourite theories in his presence. It was a rare and disagreeable experience for the shrewd old man to be subjected to the scrutiny of a person almost as perceptive as himself. He was human enough to prefer the company of his disciples although he knew they flattered him outrageously. He avenged himself upon his spiky young friend by criticizing his tendency in his writing 'to fly at everything like a rooster', by accusing him of using stylistic gimmicks and by telling him disagreeable home truths such as that a romantic like him could never be a socialist—'all romantics are monarchists'. From time to time Gorky betrays in his notes how he bridled at the great man's sallies: 'He is the devil and I am still an infant, he must not touch me'—'I very much doubt if I am more bookish than he.'

The relationships between Tolstoy and Chekhov and Tolstoy and Sulerzhitsky, as Gorky presents them, are marked by an ease and lack of restraint which distinguish them from that which prevails between the two principals in this dramatic fragment. Tolstoy greatly admired Chekhov as a writer and he praised him openly although this embarrassed his modest friend—'smiling affectionately he put his arms around A. P.'s shoulder, and the latter, covered in confusion, began to talk in a deep voice about his dacha, about the Tartars.' Sulerzhitsky's slightly effeminate personality seems to have appealed to that part of Tolstoy's intensely masculine nature which understood so well the feminine principle in humanity. The two of them throughout Gorky's memoir argue about everything but remain the best of friends, although Tolstoy disliked being contradicted.

Mutually wary, and not completely at ease in each other's presence, Tolstoy and Gorky nevertheless perceived that they shared a profound sense of outrage that the world was not ordered as they wished it to be; Gorky writes of Tolstoy—'an age-old Russian type reduced to passive anarchism by the fruitlessness of his numerous attempts to construct a more truly human life on earth'; Tolstoy told Gorky: 'You are by nature a believer and you cannot get on without God. You will soon realise this. But you do not believe out of stubbornness, from a feeling of offence because the world is not fashioned as you think it ought to be.' Something has already been said in this book of the characteristically Russian quality of *ozorstvo* manifested by the urchin of Nizhny Novgorod, Alexei Peshkov, and later transmitted by him to some of his fictional heroes; as M. Gorky, the famous writer, this urchin meets the greatest Russian of his time and discovers in him the same feeling of frustrated resentment at the world's imperfections which he was aware of (and admired) in himself. It is, of course, deceptively easy for a man to detect his own characteristics in another man whom he profoundly respects. Much in Tolstoy's life, thought, and work, however, fits Gorky's intuitive divination of him as a type of Russian *ozornik*, similar to himself. Gorky himself attributes Tolstoy's debunking of Dante and Shakespeare to the element of *ozorstvo* in his nature—he took pleasure, Gorky thought, in casting down the idols of mankind because mankind obstinately refused to observe Tolstoyan standards of morality.

Reading Gorky's sketch we gradually realize that its excellence springs from almost perfect harmony of style and content. Tolstoy was a man of such a diverse and contradictory personality, and each facet of his personality appeared and disappeared with such bewildering speed before the eyes of an observer, that he was the ideal subject for the dramatic, impressionistic memoir of a human being in which Gorky excelled. We see in Gorky's sketch not only the writer and thinker but the whole man, his physical reality, his opinions, and his personality all fused into a single unforgettable picture in which the writer makes no attempt to explain away the contradictions which made

Tolstoy what he was, as man and artist, but simply presents them in his everyday behaviour. Thus we see Tolstoy, who strove all his life to achieve humility, treat with aristocratic disdain a Moscow manufacturer who because he had heard him described as an anarchist ventured to address him familiarly. Gorky's comment on this incident is typical of his manner of writing—he says nothing of the obvious contradiction in Tolstoy's behaviour but makes an acid remark about the manufacturer: 'This man was a large-scale wealthy factory-owner, he possessed a considerable stomach and a fleshy, meat-coloured face—why did he want Tolstoy to be an anarchist? One of the "profound mysteries" of the Russian soul.'

In his sketch Gorky's hostility to Tolstoyan moral teaching is felt in the tension underlying their relationship. He makes this hostility explicit in the first part of his letter to Korolenko, inspired by the report of Tolstoy's flight. We should recall that in 1910, when this letter was written, the political reaction in Russia which followed the abortive revolution of 1905 was at its height and many members of the intelligentsia had once more become absorbed by Tolstoyan theories of personal life. From Capri Gorky observed this new vogue for self-perfection and non-resistance to evil with dismay. In his letter he expresses one of his most typical ideas about Tolstoy—that realizing the weakness of much of his teaching he longed, in the manner of the ancient Russian saints, to suffer in order to increase his authority over men's minds. He wished to leave behind him the impression of a suffering saint and his flight from his family (Gorky declares) was a last desperate attempt to impose this impression upon posterity. Gorky watched with indignation as the great man's disciples set about working out what he regarded as their master's cunning design. Vitriolically he writes: 'The newspapers have arrived and it is already clear that people in Russia have begun "to manufacture a legend"—once upon a time there lived a crowd of idlers and timewasters and they concocted for themselves a saint.' In his memoir of Countess Tolstoy Gorky declares his conviction that Tolstoy the great artist always looked askance at Tolstoy the moralist and in his letter to Korolenko he remarks that Tolstoyan rules of life were in his view what the great man 'had left over' from his unceasing mental struggle to solve the only problem which really interested him—the meaning of his own death. Ordinary mortals looked to him for moral guidance and the rules were the best he could do for them. Having formulated them he could then return to meditation upon his personal destiny, leaving his disciples to spread his teaching. His inborn spiritual despotism made him wish to impose this teaching upon people although the rational side of his nature doubted its validity. This being so, thought Gorky, its unconditional acceptance by many intellectuals who should have been concerning themselves with the liberation of Russia from Tsarism was all the more monstrous.

In our treatment of the play *The Lower Depths* we shall see the creative use made by Gorky of his view of Tolstoyan moral teaching. Gorky was never a detached thinker and his antipathy to Tolstoyanism undoubtedly sprang in large part from his dislike of the Tolstoyans he chanced to meet. He was, nevertheless, right in believing that the ideas of great men can become harmful when they are taken up by cranks, publicity seekers, and sycophants. He particularly resented the propagation of Tolstoyan moral tenets because in his view they corrupted the image of what he knew Tolstoy to be—not a saint but an imperfect human being of miraculous genius of whom the rest of mankind (and especially Russians) should be unashamedly proud. When he received the slightly premature news of Tolstoy's death all thoughts of the harmfulness of Tolstoyanism left him and he could think only of the grievous loss the world had suffered. The second part of his letter to Korolenko is a lyrical elegy of profound and burning pathos; pride at having known such a man, wonderment that he existed, grief that the earth no longer possesses him—all mingle in the moving farewell of a man of humble birth and lesser talent to the proud nobleman whose genius had for more than half a century graced Russian letters. The reader feels that Gorky regards Tolstoy as a fabulous hero of the Russian land, like the superhuman heroes of the ancient *byliny*—folk epics—which he loved.

As interesting in a different way as Gorky's sketch of Tolstoy is his memoir of the millionaire barge-owner of Nizhny Novgorod, Nikolai Bugrov, an ancestral merchant who was as characteristic of his social type as Tolstoy in many ways was characteristic of the old Russian landowner. Bugrov died in the same year as Tolstoy, 1910. Gorky's attitude to him was similar to his attitude to the great writer —a mixture of admiration, curiosity, and disapproval. Bugrov was greatly taken with Gorky's fictional merchant Yakov Mayakin, and told him that although he personally had never met a man exactly like him, he was sure he must exist somewhere.

Bugrov differed from Mayakin in that he suffered from attacks of restlessness and fits of remorse for his commercial misdeeds which prompted him to contribute large sums of money to charitable purposes. He used to say that he could never understand why he was subject to such soul-searching, because his family had always been rich and he was therefore undivided in his class loyalty. He was intrigued by his talented young fellow-townsman, but disapproved of the spirit of rebellion in his work; a writer's task, he would say, was to tell stories and not to cause disruption (*rasskazyvat i ne razvyazyvat*).

The best and most striking sketch in the collection *Through Russia* is the first, 'The Birth of a Man', which was published in the magazine *Legacies* for April 1912. It is based upon a real adventure which befell Gorky in the summer of 1892 during the famine of that year.

'The Birth of a Man' describes how Gorky, as a twenty-
three-year-old youth, once helped a woman to give birth to
a baby boy by the side of the road between Sukhum and
Ochenchiri in the Caucasus. Her husband had died in
Sukhum and with four other men she was tramping to
Ochenchiri in search of food and work when the birth over-
took her. Her companions abandoned her because of their
desperate need to find food and Gorky came upon her
attracted by her cries of pain. Together they succeeded in
bringing forth the child.

On several occasions in his work Tolstoy describes at
length a character's moment of death. It is typical of Gorky
that he should have chosen to describe not the death but
the birth of a man. The title of his sketch is emotionally
charged, expressing both his delight in the gift of life and
his sense of the supreme value of a human being.

Few writers can have composed as stark a picture of
physical suffering as Gorky presents in his description of
the woman's efforts to give birth to her child with only his
inexpert assistance. 'Scoring the earth with her fingers,
uprooting tufts of withered grass and struggling to thrust
them into her mouth, scattering soil over her terrifying,
inhumanly contorted face and bloodshot eyes, the woman
writhed like a strip of birch bark in a forest fire.' Few writers
again can have written with greater joy of the safe delivery
of a child whose receipt of life is the reward of its mother's
agony. The second part of this sketch is a sustained hymn
to life and to maternal love, counterbalancing the grim
testimony of the first to the pain and anguish which human
beings may be called upon to endure. It delights Gorky to
show that the woman's suffering had a positive purpose.

Generally speaking, the sketches in *Through Russia* and
Notes from my Diary do not add a great deal to what in
other works Gorky had already told us about Russian people
as he knew them. 'The Ice-breaker' in the first series resembles the stories 'Vanka Mazin' and 'Kirilka' in that the

central figure, Osip, a foreman joiner, in a single dramatic incident unexpectedly reveals qualities of courage and resource which contrast sharply with the general tenor of his personality—he is a garrulous, cynical, crafty, and dishonest old man. It is typical of Gorky's presentation of the behaviour of lower-class Russian people that acts of kindness, heroism, or self-sacrifice usually occur without warning or preparation, erupting suddenly in the middle of a pattern of existence compounded of stupidity, brutality, and the indulgence of animal appetites. At great risk to his life Osip leads his party of seven across disintegrating ice for no other reason than that they wish to take part in the Easter festivities which have been arranged on the other bank of the river. Gorky here shows how a trivial purpose inspires an ignorant Russian peasant to perform a great feat of leadership; of what deeds, the reader wonders, might Osip and his like be capable if life offered them a really serious task?

Notes from my Diary suffers from the defect that most of its contents are what Gorky himself called, in another place, 'literature about the sixth finger', that is, about people who are in some way abnormal, either physically or psychologically. Two typical characters in the book are the religious maniac Anna Schmidt, who believes herself to be a reincarnation of Mary Magdalene, and the locksmith Kortsov, who makes a lock which discharges a bullet into the face of anyone who opens it. In general this series of sketches is good journalism, written in a lighter style than the majority of Gorky's work, but made up of material which is largely anecdotal. Curiosity about eccentric or totally deranged human beings was one more characteristic which Gorky shared with his arch ideological enemy, Dostoevsky. A truly Dostoevskian character in *Notes from my Diary* is the peasant Merkulov, who becomes so obsessed with the notion of how easy it is to take life that he commits three murders and then suicide.

5. PLAYS

GORKY's plays, although numerous, have added little to his reputation as a writer. In Russia itself only three, *The Lower Depths*, *Vassa Zheleznova*, and *Yegor Bulychov and the Others*, have enjoyed any degree of popularity, and of these only *The Lower Depths* is known internationally.

The idea for *The Lower Depths* was first conceived by Gorky in 1900. He began the writing of it at the end of 1901 while he was living in the Crimea and finished it in the middle of June 1902 in Arzamas. It was first presented in the Moscow Arts Theatre on the 18th of December 1902.

The central character of *The Lower Depths* and the one who has been most variously interpreted by successive actors, is Luka, the wandering sage who enters the action at the end of the first act and disappears suddenly at the end of the third. During the winter and spring of 1901-2, while he was writing his play, Gorky as we have seen lived in the Crimea on terms of close acquaintanceship with Tolstoy. It would be an exaggeration to say that the figure of Luka was suggested to him by Tolstoy, because wandering philosophers occur in certain of his other works (for example the religious sectarian A. V. Ryabinin, who spends some time in Salabanova's icon-painting workshop in *My Apprenticeship*), and he was interested in them as national types. The influence of Gorky's particular view of Tolstoy upon his concept of Luka is, however, unmistakable. Gorky, as we have seen, regarded Tolstoyan theories of self-perfection, self-simplification, and non-resistance to evil as spiritual opiates through which the great man encouraged thinking people to devote their attention to problems of personal life instead of to revolutionary activity; Luka appears

from nowhere in the dark dosshouse of the brutal, tyrannical
Mikhail Kostylev, filled with human wrecks, and indulges
their fancy with dreams of escape from the unbearable reality
of their lives, instead of urging them to overthrow the tyrant
who exploits them. (Kostylev's murder by the thief Pepel
occurs suddenly, almost accidentally, and it is the result of a
personal feud and not an act of planned rebellion.) Again,
Luka offers advice and consolation liberally to the inmates of
the dosshouse and talks piously of the need to pity those who
suffer, but his words are devoid of warmth and real kindness,
and he shows less compassion for Anna Kleshch, dying of
consumption after a life of hardship and deprivation, than
some of her degraded fellow-lodgers—he merely laughs
at her when she expresses a pathetic desire to live on instead of finding what he has promised her—peace in non-
existence. In his 'Memories of Tolstoy' Gorky tells us that
Tolstoy produced upon him the impression of being altogether indifferent to his fellow-creatures, and that he
seemed to resent the thought which he felt morally con-
strained to give to their problems because he was genuinely
interested only in his own inner life. In Luka's facile
moralizing and inexhaustible flow of consoling words Gorky
wished to reproduce what he saw as Tolstoy's fundamental
lack of concern for people, which he concealed behind constant readiness to offer them moral advice. Ironically, Tolstoy himself told Gorky that he somehow could not believe
in Luka's goodheartedness. Luka is a kind of Dostoevskian
double of Tolstoy; his vagrant life is a debased version of
the great man's spiritual seeking, his gratuitous advice on
how to live the *reductio ad absurdum* of Tolstoyan moral
instruction. Tolstoy's play *The Power of Darkness* was first
presented in the Moscow Arts Theatre on 5 September
1902, not long before the *première* of *The Lower Depths*.
In Gorky's treatment of Luka the Russian theatre-going
public could not but see a polemic with the Tolstoyan
rustic sage, Akim. At that particular moment in Russian

history, only three years before the revolution of 1905, Gorky feared that the influence of Tolstoyan moral preoccupations upon thinking people might weaken their determination to overthrow Tsarism. This was one reason why he showed Kostylev's lodgers as more desperately unhappy after Luka has seduced them with his advice and solace, then disappeared, than they were before he came. If people listen to such men as Luka, who spread harmful forms of moral teaching, they will escape from evil surroundings only in fancy, and when reality once more closes in upon them, it will seem to them more unbearable than before. At the highest level Luka is linked with Tolstoy, on a lower plane he shows kinship with the vagrant religious schismatics who, convinced of the sinfulness of the contemporary Russian state, wandered to all corners of the land searching for a place where they believed pure Christian truth was still to be found. This kinship is most clearly expressed in the story of 'the true, just land' which in the third act of the play Luka tells the cynic Bubnov in an attempt to persuade him that human beings cannot live without illusions—once, he relates, a man believed implicitly in this land, but when a scientist proved conclusively to him that it did not exist he hanged himself. One dream of this spiritual Utopia cherished among the schismatics was that it was a place where there was no theft, no murder, and no greed. One cannot dissociate such a dream from the Gorkian vision of a social order based upon perfect justice and equality. This is why, despite their fundamental hostility, the reader senses a certain undertone of sympathy between Luka and his principal philosophical enemy in the play, the ex-convict Satin. Gorky disapproves of the nature of the illusions with which Luka consoles the lodgers, but he approves of the purpose for which he invents them—to make Kostylev's victims believe in the possibility of the existence of something good outside his foul den.

At the same time as *The Lower Depths* was maturing in Gorky's mind, he was reflecting upon the two sketches which he eventually wrote in 1903 under the titles 'Notes on the petty bourgeois mentality' and 'Man'. His concept of Luka is linked with the first sketch because, as we have seen, he considered that Tolstoyan moral teaching encouraged the political apathy which he saw as one of the distinguishing characteristics of the petty *bourgeois*. He presents his ideal, symbolic figure 'Man' as the enemy of every manifestation of the petty *bourgeois* mentality. In his play he embodies this ideal figure in the chivalrous, freedom-loving Satin. Throughout the action of *The Lower Depths* Satin mocks at and derides the seductive promises of happiness in other places with which Luka captivates the imagination of his fellow down-and-outs; and in the fourth act, after Luka has disappeared, he angrily condemns his consoling lies as 'the religion of slaves and bosses'—an opiate for the former and an instrument of exploitation for the latter. 'Truth', he proclaims passionately, 'is the God of the free man.'

The symbolic conflict between Luka's view of the manner in which people should face misfortune and that of Satin is the fundamental dramatic theme of *The Lower Depths*. The presence of this conflict dominates the action, although Satin plays a relatively small part in the conversations and discussions which make up the first three acts. He began his descent to the social depths through being sentenced to five years in jail for murdering a man in defence of his sister: for him, therefore, love of truth means ability to face the fact that a malevolent destiny has destroyed his life, without asking for compassion or consolation from other people. He remains totally impervious to Luka's soothing words, even in the third act, when the latter's influence upon the other characters reaches its peak. He is the only one of Kostylev's lodgers who is the same person at the end of the play, after Luke has come and gone, as he was at the beginning. Never having believed the old man's consoling lies, he does not suffer the pain of disillusionment experienced by the Actor and the prostitute Nastya when they realize that their comforter was a charlatan. He is never persuaded, like Pepel and Natasha, that happiness is within his grasp, only to see his hopes cruelly dashed.

In Gorky's play, as we have seen, Satin is not only an individual but also the champion of a philosophy of life; the author attempts to reconcile his two identities by making him proclaim his own courage in adversity as the greatest virtue of the human spirit. Nevertheless, Gorky encountered a formidable artistic difficulty when he set out to portray, in the same character, on the one hand a down-and-out defeated by life and on the other a rebellious idealist who proclaims that work is noble when it gives pleasure, that the word 'Man' has a proud ring, and that the oppressed should not forgive their persecutors, but should fight back. Gorky revealed his disquiet at this ambivalence in a letter to K. A. Pyatnitsky dated 15 July 1902, in which he said that Satin's speech extolling Man 'sounded out of place in his mouth', but that no other character in the play was suited to make it. In an attempt to overcome this incongruity the author made Satin into a man who deliberately chooses to live in a dosshouse because of an anarchical illusion that he can find absolute freedom there, and whose rags conceal a nature still as chivalrous and as independent as it was at the time he committed the crime which precipitated his ruin. His chivalrous instinct asserts itself in the fourth act when he protects Nastya against a threatened assault by Baron. The character most akin to him in the rest of Gorky's work is probably the noble-minded, atheistic icon-painter Sitanov in *My Apprenticeship*, but he is also in certain respects similar to Chelkash, especially in his contempt for servile toil.

Within the framework of the main dramatic theme of *The Lower Depths*—the philosophical conflict between Luka

and Satin—several minor dramas are played out concerning
the influence of Luka's consoling words upon other inmates
of the dosshouse. Anna Kleshch is on the point of death
from consumption when he arrives, and she dies towards
the end of the second act. The burden of Luka's advice to
her is that if she can only endure a little more suffering in
this life she will find comfort in the next. The pathos of her
situation is that she has known so much hardship on earth
that even the promise of peace in non-existence consoles
her. Death saves her from the Actor's bitter disillusionment.
In the play she is the representative of all the suffering
humanity who fill the pages of Gorky's other works, and in
the attitude of the other characters to her he reverts to a
subject which always concerned him—the question as to
whether or not people should extend compassion to those
who suffer. Bubnov, Baron, Satin, and Anna's husband
Kleshch behave mercilessly towards her, but the Actor,
Kvashnya, and Natasha are moved to pity by her plight.
Luka comforts her because he thinks that all human beings
need compassion. For Satin compassion lowers men's
dignity and encourages them to accept suffering too readily.
As we have seen (page 84) Gorky never reached a definite
conclusion about which of these two views he supported.
This is another reason for his ambivalent attitude to the
two main characters in his play.

　In the story 'Twenty-Six Men and a Girl' Gorky shows
that to people whose lives are dominated by hardship,
suffering, and deprivation a consoling illusion may bring
temporary joy, but that after the bitter truth has destroyed
this illusion they find reality harder to endure than before
they conceived it. From his autobiographical novels we
know that Gorky culled this idea from his own inner life;
in *The Lower Depths* he dramatizes it in the fate of the
Actor. When the play opens the Actor is an apparently
hopeless alcoholic, but he finds his condition bearable and
even takes some degree of masochistic pleasure in it. Luka

persuades him that 'in a certain town' there is a hospital where he will be cured of his alcoholism free of charge and then be able to begin a new life. Previously resigned to his fate, the Actor finds the prospect of starting life anew so captivating that in his imagination he endows the legendary hospital with a magnificence undreamed of by Luka himself. 'A splendid hospital [he tells Natasha]—marble everywhere, marble floors, bright, clean rooms, food, and everything free.' In the fourth act, after Luka's mysterious disappearance, the Actor strives desperately to preserve his belief in the hospital, despite Satin's and Baron's scornful denials of its existence, because he has created a whole imaginary life in the future around it. We realize that his illusion is slipping from him when he asks the Tartar to pray for him. The play ends with Baron's dramatic announcement that he has hanged himself on a neighbouring vacant site. He had the strength to endure the tortures of alcoholism, but his spirit was completely broken by the annihilation of the unexpected hope which Luka had given him that he might recover from it. Similarly, the bakers in 'Twenty-Six Men and a Girl' bore patiently their grim life in the underground bakery, but suffered an agonizing sense of loss when their belief in the purity of their beloved Tanya proved to be unfounded.

Nastya, the prostitute in *The Lower Depths*, is linked with the prostitute Teresa in the story 'Boles'—they both invent a lover whose imaginary existence makes their sordid lives bearable. Luka does not invent Nastya's illusion that she has known a great love in her life, but he encourages her to cherish it in the face of the scornful incredulity of Baron and Bubnov. In the story Teresa refuses to renounce her illusory lover, although she knows that her student friend who writes her letters to him is aware that he does not exist; and they both persevere in their game of pretence. In the play, however, Gorky carries this situation one step further. Luka is for Nastya what the student was for Teresa—a person who understands why she needs her illusion—and when he disappears she is left defenceless against the renewed taunts of the others, and is obliged at last to confess to herself that her lover does not exist. She contrasts the real people around her with the imaginary figure in whom she can no longer believe and showers them with vitriolic abuse. 'I wish someone would pack you all off to Siberia or sweep you like dirt into a hole somewhere.' Her fate is less tragic than the Actor's, but reveals, like his, that people who allow themselves to be lulled for a short while by a consoling lie find reality more bitter when this lie is exposed than they would have found it had they faced up to it from the start.

In the novel *Paul the Wretched* and the story 'Red Vaska' (1899) Gorky shows how two men and two women fall sincerely in love, but do not marry because their past experience of life has been so bitter that they cannot envisage the possibility of happiness together. In *The Lower Depths* the thief Vasili Pepel and Kostylev's sister Natasha also fall in love, but Natasha has known only ill-treatment from her relatives, and no one has ever called Pepel anything but thief, and in consequence, like their predecessors in Gorky's work, they cannot convince themselves that, if they marry, life together will be better than each has known it separately. As with Nastya, Gorky takes this situation from his story one step further in his play through the agency of Luka. Luka takes upon himself the task of urging Natasha and Pepel to leave their present life behind and to look for happiness in Siberia, where much useful work remains to be done. He convinces Natasha that Pepel will respect her if they marry, and Pepel that once married he will be able to live as an honest man, and towards the end of the third act he achieves his purpose of persuading them to entrust their happiness to each other. This marks the peak of his influence with the inmates of the dosshouse. Before this point Pepel has been one of the most strenuous opponents of Luka's cult of the consoling lie, but he now yields to the natural desire of his soul for happiness and fulfilment in a successful human relationship accompanied by worthwhile work. His dream, however, is rudely shattered. Vasilisa Kostyleva, who is in love with him, and her husband pour boiling water over Natasha's feet to prevent them from going away together, and Pepel in revenge murders Kostylev. He is imprisoned, and Natasha disappears from the house. Pursuing under Luka's influence the mirage of happiness, they have succeeded only in destroying its possibility for themselves for ever.

Luka's consoling lies in *The Lower Depths* are contested not only by the chivalrous ex-convict Satin but also, with equal vehemence, by the cynical ex-fur-merchant Bubnov. Satin, however, despises Luka's fantasies because he considers that to listen to empty words of consolation in adversity, instead of fighting to overcome it, degrades mankind; Bubnov, on the other hand, is not concerned about the fact that Luka's seductive promises may undermine his fellow-lodgers' desire to break out of Kostylev's power,— he demolishes them for the sake of the malevolent pleasure he finds in doing so. He does not, like Satin, respect truth as an ideal to which to aspire, but equates truth with reality which he sees as a set of unpleasant facts. Satin's abhorrence of compassion springs from his conviction that to pity men reveals a lack of faith in their ability to create their own happiness; Bubnov refuses to feel compassion for Anna because death is a fact for all people. 'It's the same for everyone,' he says to Natasha, 'they are born, live a while, then die. I'll die, just like you. . . . What's there to be sorry about?' Akin to Bubnov in his view of life as a collection of irrefutable, disagreeable facts is the locksmith Kleshch, Anna's husband. For him truth amounts to the fact that a man loses his arm through an industrial accident or that an expert craftsman like himself cannot find work and sinks to the level of the other inmates of the dosshouse, whom he despises. The change which takes place in Kleshch in the course of the play lies in his slow, unwilling acceptance of the fact of the loss of his workman's dignity. His descent to the degradation of the gutter recalls the fate of Grigori Orlov the skilled cobbler. Kleshch of all Kostylev's lodgers most richly deserves compassion, because he does not dream of escape from the depths through a miracle, but plans to achieve it by means of hard work and yields only when he realizes that this most reasonable of all purposes, because of social conditions, cannot be fulfilled. In the years of industrial recession 1899–1903 such men as Kleshch, wishing to work but unable to find jobs, would strike a chord with the audience.

When *The Lower Depths* was first presented most critics regarded it as a static play, a series of sketches from life without internal links, a naturalistic work almost devoid of action and dramatic conflicts. The German critic F. Mering, in an article written in 1934, strongly supported this view, declaring that the only semblance of conflict lay in the relationship between Kostylev and Pepel, that the play therefore was completed in the third act with Kostylev's murder, and that the fourth act was superfluous. Chekhov to a certain extent had shared this opinion, and in a letter to Gorky dated 29 July 1902 he enthusiastically praised the second act, but criticized the fourth because, he said, Gorky had removed from it all the interesting characters except the Actor, and he declared further that the Actor's suicide was not sufficiently prepared. The opinion of Mering and the critics who thought like him can be explained by the fact that in the play they were interested only in the emotions of love and jealousy which are the conventional ingredients of drama; and Chekhov's antipathy to the fourth act sprang from his aversion to Gorky's tendency, as he put it, 'to mount the pulpit and read his apostolic letters to his congregation in an ecclesiastical tone of voice'. Clearly, Kostylev's murder is only a subordinate incident in the unfolding of the main dramatic theme of the play, the destruction of illusions by reality and the influence of their destruction upon those who cherish them; the murder is a catastrophe which marks the apogee of Luka's influence upon the lodgers but which at the same time brings about his sudden disappearance at the height of the scuffle which his interference in the affairs of Natasha and Pepel has provoked. This catastrophe at the end of the third act is followed by the denouement of the fourth, in which Gorky completes the ideological pattern of his play by juxtaposing Satin's concept of Man with Luka's, and at the same time shows the baleful results of Luka's abortive attempts at consolation upon the state of mind of those who listened to him. With his criticism, however, Gorky mingles grief at Luka's failure. The stage is dark, as if in mourning for shattered hopes.

To a certain extent the way for the Actor's suicide is prepared by Luka's tale, in the third act, of the man who hanged himself when it was proved to him that the 'true and just land' did not exist. The Actor's suicide is also the culminating point of all that has preceded it in the fourth act. We have heard that Natasha has disappeared and that Pepel will go to jail, Kleshch has given up his struggle to remain an honest workman, and Nastya has given way to bitterness. The dramatic impact upon the spectator of Satin's pronouncement of his religion of freedom and the dignity of Man is enhanced by the Actor's suicide—the second catastrophe of the play to be caused by the interference of Luka, Satin's ideological enemy, in the affairs of the doss-house. Chekov, however, was more impressed by the catastrophes than by Satin's oratory. 'In any event', he wrote to Gorky after reading the play, 'you can say goodbye to your reputation as an optimist.' Truly, Satin's high-sounding words only repeat the romantic sentiments of the ragged heroes of Gorky's early stories, and the writer seemed to have parted company with the latter four years before when in the story 'Creatures That Once Were Men' he showed the swashbuckling Kuvalda packed off to jail by the commercial establishment. Stanislavsky found difficulty in uttering Satin's tendentious speeches about Man in a convincing manner, and he confesses that he fell into the sin of theatricality in trying to do so. 'I overacted romanticism and fell into banal theatrical pathos and declamation.' Gorky's rhetoric, indeed, taxed the skill of every member of the Moscow Arts Theatre as they tried to utter it naturally and sincerely. It evoked a warm response among the audiences, but this was because they were already spiritually prepared for the great revolution in the cause of freedom which lay only three years in the future.

Yegor Bulychov and the Others was written in 1932 and first presented on 6 November 1933 by the Leningrad State Theatre; on 25 November it was presented in Moscow by the Vakhtangov Theatre. This play is a dramatic study of the behaviour of the central character, Yegor Bulychov, a timber merchant of Kostroma, during the last months of his life, which also happen to be the last months of the Tsarist régime. His death from cancer of the liver coincides with the beginning of the March revolution of 1917.

Gorky's play resembles Tolstoy's story 'The Death of Ivan Ilich' in that in both the imminence of death makes the central character look back critically upon his life, which by worldly standards has been an unqualified success but which during his last illness he comes to regard in a quite different light. Bulychov's situation further resembles that of Ilich because both are keenly aware that the members of their households are more concerned about the inheritance they are shortly to receive than about the suffering of the sick man. In the play this concern divides Bulychov's family into two warring groups who do not trouble to conceal their intrigues in his presence. Both Bulychov and Ivan Ilich find in their relatives' greed support for their growing conviction that they have spent their lives in an immoral social sphere. In Tolstoy's story only the peasant Gerasim shows his master any degree of compassion, thus reflecting the writer's view that goodness was to be found only among the simplest people. In Gorky's play Bulychov also receives sincere compassion in his plight only from those characters who command the author's personal sympathy—the sick man's illegitimate daughter Shura, his mistress the maid Glasha, and his godson the Bolshevik Yakov Laptev. Each one of these three stands outside Bulychov's social class, and the natural affinity which they feel for him, and he for them, underlines his alienation from this class. In varying degrees each of them is on the side of the approaching revolution.

Bulychov is as keenly aware that an unavoidable social cataclysm is at hand in Russia as he is of the certainty of his own imminent death. He rebels against both because of the strong individualism of his nature. He is willing that all other human beings should suffer the common fate of death, so long as he personally is spared it; he approves the approach of a revolution which will destroy the power and prosperity of the kind of people who surround him, but he abhors the possibility that it will also demolish the business which was his personal creation. He painfully realizes that if a political upheaval engulfs his business, no part of him will survive his death. This realization inspires the tragic pathos of the coincidence of the end of his life with the annihilation of Russian capitalism. In no work has Gorky exploited the encroachment of the events of 1917 upon personal destiny with greater artistic effect.

Bulychov's closest spiritual kinsman in Gorky's earlier work is Ignat Gordeev. Both from humble beginnings acquire considerable wealth through successful commercial activity, and both feel themselves temperamentally at odds with the mercantile society into which their career brings them. It is not moral fastidiousness which makes them wonder if in commerce they have chosen the right way of life, but profound uncertainty as to whether they could not have devoted their great energies to some better purpose, which they might have fulfilled among people more spiritually akin to them. Gorky says of Gordeev that he never questioned the rightness of his own actions, and even on the brink of death Bulychov is unrepentant of his past misdeeds, both in his private and in his commercial life. 'I'm a sinner', he exclaims, 'I've wronged people and I've sinned in every way. Well, all people wrong each other and it can't be helped, such is life.' Unlike Gordeev Bulychov lives to the eve of a great proletarian revolution, and it is this fact which is the most virulent element of his bitter sense of having somehow lost his way in life—the class into which he was born but which he deserted in order to accumulate a private fortune is about to assert itself in his native land and to seize back his wealth—but it is too late for him to rejoin it.

In their strength and their contradictions Gordeev and Bulychov have close affinities with the textile millionaire Savva Morozov. This man was the descendant of a serf who in 1797, with his master's permission, founded a small ribbon factory and in 1820 bought his family's freedom at the cost of 17,000 roubles. Gorky first met Morozov in 1896 at the great industrial exhibition of that year in Nizhny Novgorod and was greatly impressed by his apparent determination to seize political power for his social class. When, however, the two met again in 1901, Gorky discovered that his initial impression of the industrialist had been superficial and over-simplified, and that far from being a typical factory owner, sure of himself and his class, Morozov was at odds with himself and despised his family and his commercial background. This dichotomy manifested itself in a number of different ways: Morozov permitted the calling out of troops to take punitive action against strikers in his works, although at the same time he was contributing funds to the publication of revolutionary literature; he tried to play the part of a leader of the

Russian *bourgeoisie* although he concealed the Bolshevik
Bauman from the gendarmerie in his own flat; he spoke
of the inevitability and the necessity of a revolutionary
upheaval in Russia and seemed to desire it, but at the height
of the events of 1905, on 13 May of that year, he committed
suicide in Vichy in France. In this play Gorky has succeeded in catching some part of the tragic conflicts of this
man's life, and of the lives of many similar men of smaller
stature.

Gorky wrote the play *Vassa Zheleznova* in 1910, and it
was first presented by Nezlobin's theatre in Moscow on
21 February 1911. He completely revised it twenty years
later. In the first version, the heroine, Vassa Zheleznova,
the mother of a commercial family, is depicted simply as a
monster consumed with lust for the acquistion of money
and property which distorts all human feelings in her. The
appearance of the play provoked critical comparisons of
Gorky's 'two mothers', Vlasova and Zheleznova, which
dwelt predominantly upon the difference in the nature of
the two women's love for their children. In the revised version Gorky softened somewhat the repellent figure of the
original play and succeeded in investing her with a certain
note of tragedy. In order to achieve her aim of gathering all
the resources of the family business into her hands, she
uses her milksop, impotent son, Pavel, as a tool to bring
about the death of her brother-in-law, Prokhor Zheleznov,
and then disposes of him by making him enter a monastery
to atone for his sin. At the end of the play her daughter
Anna and daughter-in-law Lyudmila take pity upon her in
her loneliness and promise to help her in her management
of the business without male assistance. She promises that
their children will be her heirs.

Vassa Zheleznova is composed of the traditional dramatic
ingredients of greed, love, jealousy, murder, and suicide
and it is Gorky's most successful play of this type. The
characterization has a certain strength which compensates

for the complexity of the plot. As she appears in the final version, Vassa merits comparison with Schedrin's Arina Fyodorovna Golovlyova. The conflicts between the characters are soundly motivated, springing from fundamental clashes of temperament and of material interest which are lacking in the Gorkian plays of ideas.

AFTERWORD

As a writer Gorky inherited many of the traditions of nineteenth-century Russian critical realism. He is linked with the romantic strain in the work of Pushkin and Lermontov through his love for the wild, majestic scenery of the Caucasus and the southern steppe in which he finds refuge from the squalid, commercial way of life of the towns of the middle and lower Volga region, just as his great predecessors fled there from the false, fashionable life of the capitals. Gorky, like Pushkin, felt profound sympathy for the age-old natural wisdom of the nomadic steppe-dwellers, and he shared Lermontov's desire to create the figure of a romantic superman to set in contrast to the average petty-minded urban citizen of his time. Like Lermontov he brought his romantic hero to fictional life but was compelled by artistic integrity to point to the weaknesses in his nature which prevented him from being a hero in the real world. With Gogol Gorky shares moral disapproval of contemporary society and, as the reverse side of this disapproval, shows great respect for past ages when the human personality was whole and the gigantic achievements of mankind's artistic genius mirrored this wholeness. It is significant that both Gogol and Gorky cherished great affection for Italy. With Goncharov Gorky had in common a keen awareness of the baleful influence which the sleepy, stagnant way of life of Russian provincial towns had exercised upon the national psychology and, although he lacks his predecessor's involuntary affection for this life, nevertheless in his depiction of the Oblomov-like Matvei Kozhemyakin he shows Goncharov's compassion for the people whom through the centuries it had spiritually ruined. Much has been said in this book about Gorky's links with Tolstoy and Dostoevsky. As a creative artist Gorky must be assigned a relatively modest place among the great figures of nineteenth-century Russian literature. The somewhat jaundiced tone of Ivan Bunin's memoir of Gorky, written in 1936, sprang from the author's violent resentment of the fact that his contemporary's enormous fame had always outstripped his talent. At the turn of the century, having written only a handful of good short stories, Gorky, both in Russia and the West, enjoyed a repute almost comparable with that of Chekhov and Tolstoy. Of his subsequent work only *Childhood*, 'Memories of Tolstoy' and possibly *The Lower Depths* may incontestably be termed great, yet since October 1927, when the Communist Academy declared him to be a true proletarian writer, Soviet critics and scholars have elevated him into a major figure of world literature. At the present time many educated people in the West who do not know the name of Goncharov would cite Maxim Gorky as a Russian writer of the first rank.

Maxim Gorky is a literary phenomenon. At two different points in Russian history his name has been surrounded by an aura of glory unjustified by his artistic achievement. It is useful to look at some of the reasons for this. The great impact made by Gorky's stories upon the Russian reading public at the beginning of the eighteen-nineties can be understood if we consider three stories which enjoyed considerable popularity during the preceding fifteen years. These stories are 'Four Days' (1877) and 'The Red Flower' (1879) by Vsevolod Garshin and Tolstoy's 'The Death of Ivan Ilich' (1885).

'Four Days' describes how a Russian soldier during the Russo-Turkish war of 1876–7 kills a Turk and is himself gravely wounded by his victim; unable to move, the Russian lies helpless beside the rotting corpse of the Turk for four days until he is rescued. 'The Red Flower' tells of a man so morbidly sensitive to suffering and evil that he goes mad and is confined in a lunatic asylum; while there he sees outside his window a number of red flowers in which he begins to imagine that all the evil in the world is concentrated; he cannot rest until by plucking these flowers he has rid the world of evil, but as he plucks the first he suffers a nervous seizure and dies. 'The Death of Ivan Ilich' is about an eminent lawyer who dies slowly of cancer; during his illness he looks back on his life which by accepted standards has been distinguished and fruitful but in the face of death seems to him to have been trivial and devoted to self-seeking. He dies happily because at the last moment he undergoes a typically Tolstoyan conversion to renunciation of self.

These three stories have certain features in common. The heroes of both of Garshin's stories are himself, because he was a man as morbidly sensitive to evil as the hero of 'The Red Flower', spent several spells in lunatic asylums, and eventually committed suicide. Hating and fearing war he felt obliged, so long as it existed, to share the sufferings of those who took part in it, and he went to the Russo-Turkish war as a volunteer. In his story the wounded soldier sees with agonizing clarity all the horror of war embodied in the putrid corpse of the man he has himself killed. To the spiritual suffering he undergoes from the contemplation of his victim is added the nausea he feels through the proximity of the corpse and the pain from his own wounds. In 'The Red Flower' Garshin exchanges the naturalistic detail of corpses on a battlefield for the grim background of a nineteenth-century Russian asylum. The ultra-sensitivity of the lunatic is expressed in the fact that when an attendant rubs his neck with a rough towel he imagines his head is being cut off. In Tolstoy's story we move from battlefield and asylum to a sick-room in which a man lies dying, suffering frightful physical pain which is comparable only to his spiritual agony as he contemplates the base manner in which he now seems to himself to have passed his time on earth.

The pleasure which Russian readers of the eighties found in these three stories indicates the unhealthy state of mind into which human beings can fall when they are languishing under severe governmental repression. Morbidity is a human failing which feeds on idleness and purposelessness, the feelings which, as we saw in the introductory chapter, tormented so many members of the Russian intelligentsia in the eighties (in fiction strikingly depicted in the figure of Dr. Chekanov in Veresaev's story 'Pathless' (1894)).

Awareness of the existence around him of evil which he feels powerless to overcome may at the same time turn the sensitive thinking person in upon himself and lend dark colours to his reflections. The fearsomeness of many of the details of physical and spiritual suffering which we find in the stories of Tolstoy and Garshin springs from this cause. Tolstoy broods upon the moral degeneracy of the new masters of post-reform Russian society, Garshin views with horror and compassion the sufferings of the underdogs, and both writers attempt to communicate their emotions to their readers through the artistic exploitation of the horrible. The intensity of Ivan Ilich's spiritual suffering reflects the intensity of Tolstoy's disapproval of the way of life of such men and the rotting corpse of Garshin's Turkish soldier together with the tortured body of the Russian who killed him give concrete form to the writer's dread of war. Thus both Tolstoy's and Garshin's exploitation of horror has personal roots. The profundity of Tolstoy's feelings may be gauged by contrasting the atmosphere of terror of his later story with the restraint and asceticism of the style of his earlier work. Some signs of this atmosphere of terror are already present in 'Anna Karenina'.

In *War and Peace* Prince Andrew lies severely wounded on Pratsensky Hill contemplating the boundless sky filled with grey drifting clouds. The sky speaks of the eternal mysteries of life and death beside which earthly preoccupations now seem to him to be meaningless and trivial. In 'Four Days' Garshin's wounded soldier lies helpless on the battlefield beside the corpse of the enemy he has killed but his mind is not concerned with cosmic issues but with the concrete problem of the meaning of war and the part of the individual in it. His world is not the infinite sky but 'only a small segment of earth, a few blades of grass, an ant crawling head-first down one of them and one or two specks of dirt from last year's greenery'. He is aghast at the murder he has committed and overwhelmed by his own physical pain—he sees war in terms of what it has meant for the Turk and himself. The contrast between Andrew's contemplation of the infinite and Garshin's hero's concern with problems of personal destiny points the difference between the ultimate preoccupations of Russian literature of the eighteen-sixties and the immediate, earthly issues which concern writers in the eighties. In the eighties even Tolstoy's horizon is narrowed.

The first words of Maxim Gorky's first story 'Makar Chudra' read: 'From the sea there blew a cold, moisture-laden wind. . . .' One can imagine the impact made by these words upon a reader accustomed for fifteen years to the kind of stories which we have just examined. At once the narrow confines of asylums and sick-rooms are broken through and the infinite expanse of the sky of *War and Peace* returns to literature in the vastness of Gorky's sea. The sea, morover, is turbulent and eternally in motion. It suggests that men should be troubled about greater issues than their personal tranquillity. Against the historical background of the early eighteen-nineties in Russia the note struck by Gorky's first story was of great significance.

In 1892, as we saw in the introductory chapter, the first signs appeared in Russian society of a widespread hardening of resistance to the repressive policy of the authorities during the eighties. From this moment on feelings of protest and rebellion spread rapidly and grow in intensity until they culminate in the revolution of 1905. As the feeling of the imminence of revolution increased in certainty, people's minds turned again to the old problem of the destiny of the Russian nation; this problem lies at the basis of Gorky's best work written during the eighteen-nineties.

The feelings of revolt and indignation which from his earliest stories inspired Gorky's work were the product of his own harsh experience during his formative years, but they faithfully echoed the rebellious mood of many of his readers. This coincidence of mood between writer and reader, combined with the novelty of the back-grounds Gorky described and of the ragged heroes he brought forward, explains much of his early popularity. His early vagrant life, of which, during the nineties, more and more became known to the vastly intrigued reading public, acquired for them symbolic significance as the expression of humanity's eternal craving for freedom—stifled by the Russian Government for a decade. The public took this new writer to their hearts as the herald of the revolutionary storm which they fervently hoped could not be long delayed. When two volumes of his collected stories appeared in 1898 their success was phenomenal.

About the year 1901 the quality of Gorky's work declined and many of his earlier admirers ceased to read him. In April 1907, after the appearance of the novel *Mother* and the play *Enemies* the critic Dimitri Filosofov wrote a famous article entitled 'The End of Gorky'. He would have been astonished to know that twenty years later these very works would inspire a new cult of Gorky in a new Russia.

The basic reason why Maxim Gorky receives such adulation in the Soviet Union lies in the fact that a new literature was necessary for the new society and of all Russian writers in any way eminent Gorky was clearly the most suitable for official elevation to the status of its founder and fountainhead. There are certain reasons why he does not fit the description of proletarian writer—he was of petty *bourgeois* origin, he was never an industrial worker, he did not describe the lives of workers, he was a religiously minded man and a romantic revolutionary who felt himself—in his own words—'to be a heretic in every party'. On the other hand certain dominant characteristics of Gorky's thought and personality harmonize perfectly with the intellectual and spiritual atmosphere of the Soviet Union. We may note first of all his burning patriotism and his absolute faith in the power of the Russian people to achieve miracles of constructive labour if their talents and energies are properly developed and exploited; linked with this faith is his reverence for all forms of education as the infallible means of bringing human ability to fruition and his exaltation of work as a force capable of transforming the condition of mankind on earth. Absolute faith in human talent and in the efficacy of work means confidence in the ability of men to conquer their environment and rejection of their need of any form of divine guidance in everyday affairs or of priestly consolation in misfortune. Human beings can find strength and solace in their sense of community with each other. Man is the be-all and end-all of existence. This was Maxim Gorky's distinctive faith, and it echoes some of the more positive elements of Soviet teaching.

Maxim Gorky believed strongly in the power of legends to influence human behaviour. His own life has proved to be more suitable than that of any other Russian writer for the creation of legends around his name. The first legend, that of the Stormy Petrel of the revolution of 1905, arose spontaneously out of the troubled mood of Russian society at the turn of the century, flourished on the eve of the revolution and now belongs to literary history; the second, that of the proletarian writer of universal genius, has been systematically created and after forty years shows no sign of decline. All in all this legend has probably done more good than harm in the land of Gorky's birth. In the highly literate country which the Soviet Union has now become, it is doubtful if it is any longer necessary. On the strength of his best work Gorky's name will survive without the support of legend.

BIBLIOGRAPHY

W. H. BRUFORD, *Chekov and his Russia*, Kegan Paul, Trench & Trubner, 1947.

B. BYALIK, *Gorky dramaturg* (*Gorky the dramatist*), Moscow, 1962.

N. A. GORCHAKOV, *The Theatre in Soviet Russia*, O.U.P., 1957.

NINA GOURFINKEL (trans. Ann Fesbach), *Gorky*, Evergreen Books, London, 1960.

I. GRUZDEV, *Gorky i ego vremya* (Vol. 1) (*Gorky and his time*), Moscow, 1948.

R. HARE, *Maxim Gorky. Romantic Realist and Conservative Revolutionary*, O.U.P., London, 1960.

A. KAUN, *Maxim Gorky and his Russia*, Jonathan Cape & Harrison Smith, N.Y., 1931.

DAN LEVIN, *Stormy Petrel: The Life and Work of Maxim Gorky*, Appleton–Century, 1965.

G. LUKACS (trans. Edith Bone), *Studies in European Realism*, Hillway Pub. Co., London, 1950.

B. V. MIKHAILOVSKY, *Dramaturgiya Gorkovo epokhi pervoy russkoy revolyutsii* (*Gorky's drama during the first Russian revolution*), Moscow, 1951.

D. S. MIRSKY, *Russia*, The Cresset Press, London, 1931.

W. E. MOSSE, *Alexander II and the Modernization of Russia*, English Universities Press, 1958.

A. I. OVCHARENKO, *Romam-epopeya M. Gorkovo, Zhizn' Klima Samgina* (Gorky's epic novel, 'The Life of Klim Samgin'), Moscow, 1965.

V. S. PRITCHETT, *The Working Novelist*, Chatto & Windus, London, 1965.

M. SLONIM, *Modern Russian Literature from Chekhov to the Present*, O.U.P., 1953.

—— *Russian Theatre*, Methuen & Co., 1961.

E. B. TAGER, *Tvorchestvo Gorkovo sovetskoi epokhi* (*Gorky's works in the Soviet period*), Moscow, 1964.

—— *Sobranie sochinenii* (*Collected Works*) (30 vols.), Moscow, 1949–55.

—— *Letopis' zhizni i tvorchestva M. Gorkovo* (*Chronicle of the life and work of M. Gorky*) (4 vols.), Moscow, 1958.

D. MACKENZIE WALLACE, *Russia* (2 vols.), Cassell & Co., 1905.

H. SETON WATSON, *The Decline of Imperial Russia*, Frederick Praeger, N.Y., 1952.

INDEX

PRINTED IN GREAT BRITAIN
AT THE UNIVERSITY PRESS, OXFORD
BY VIVIAN RIDLER
PRINTER TO THE UNIVERSITY